A DOCUMENT FOR DISCUSSION DIALOGUE AND DEBATE

Poverty and the Environment

Reconciling short-term needs with long-term sustainability goals

Contributors:

Sylvia S Tognetti, Robert Costanza,
Lourdes Arizpe, Cutler Cleveland,
Herman Daly, Anil Gupta,
Juan Martinez-Alier, Peter H May,
Mark Ritchie, Jack Ruitenbeek,
Olman Segura, Hans Opschoor
and Kanchan Chopra.

UNEP

United Nations Environment Programme

Published by United Nations Environment Programme
PO Box 30552
Nairobi, Kenya.

ISBN 92–807–1474–0

A **Banson** production
3 Turville Street
London E2 7HR

Design: Leila & Associates
Print: Lydia Litho

Acknowledgments
Research assistance for this report was provided by David Spohr, Deborah
Stein and Darrell Fruth. David Spohr and Deborah Stein also contributed to
sections of the report regarding development assistance and natural resource
accounting. Paul Scodari provided assistance in the initial stages of the report.
Comments and suggestions were provided by Marilia Pastuk, Faye Duchin,
Stephen Viederman, Richard Norgaard, Laura Cornwell and Beatrice
Castaneda. We would also like to acknowledge the helpful suggestions and
constructive criticism provided by UNEP reviewers including UNEP staff: Ann
Willcocks, H. Abaza, M. Uppenbrink, Walter Rast, Maria de Amorim, Arthur
Dahl, H. Gopalan, Hanne T. Laugeson, H. Bendahman; and Peter Hooten, The
Australian High Commission; L.S. Botero, H. Meliczak, FAO.

The front cover photograph, the *Cost of Progress* by Bhudey Bhagat, was one
of 32,000 submitted to UNEP's International Photographic Competition, *Focus
on Your World* (UNEP-Select).

TABLE OF CONTENTS

Summary   3

1 Introduction   7

The Growth of Poverty, Disparity and Environmental Degradation   7
  Poverty, Environment and Development   7
  The Development of Poverty   8
  Disparity   9
  Poverty and Environment   10
  Changing World Views   11

2 World Poverty and Environmental Degradation   16
The Nature and Extent of World Poverty   16
Measurement of Poverty   17
  Approaches used by UNDP   17
  Approaches used by the World Bank   21
  Approaches used by IFAD   23
Types, Locations and Broad Socio-economic Profile of the Poor   24
Strategies   26
The Nature and Extent of Environmental Degradation   28
  Poverty-Environment-Population Linkages   29
  Population Growth and Distribution   30
  Carrying Capacity   32
Land Degradation   34
  Desertification   35
  Deforestation   37
  Mining   40
  Loss of Biodiversity   42
  Water Quality and Supply   44
  Urbanization   48
Impacts of Environmental Stress and Resource
Exploitation on the Poor   51
  Shifting Environmental Costs to the Poor   51
  Environmental Degradation and Community Deterioration   55
The Institutionalization of Poverty and Environmental
Degradation   55
  Poverty as a Social Trap   55
  A Socio-ecological Model of Household Behaviour   56
  Developmental Repercussions   58

3 Public Policies, Poverty, and Environmental Stress   60
Policy Criteria   60
  Sustainable Scale   60
  Equitable Distribution   61
  Efficient Allocation   62
  Relationship Between the Criteria   64

Environmental Values and Income Distribution 64
International Trade and Aid Policies 66
  Exchange and Welfare 67
  Unequal Exchange 67
  Market Failures 70
  Trade and Environment Policies 71
  International Borrowing and Structural Adjustment 73
Development Assistance 78
  Multilateral Organizations 78
  The Role of Non-governmental Organizations 85
  Local Organizations 85
  An Institutional Approach towards Development 88
The Role of Women in Sustainable Development 93
Addressing Levels and Patterns of Consumption 95
Legal and Property Rights Structures 96
Community Control and Management of Common
Property Resources 99
Global Environmental and Natural Resource Agreements 99
Natural Resources and Environmental Management Policy 100
  Natural Resource Accounting 102
  Summary Natural Resource Accounts 104
  Management-Oriented Natural Resource Accounts 106
Integrated Approaches to Natural Resource Management 108

4 Conclusions and Recommendations 113

Development and Sustainability 113
Policy Recommendations 116
  Investment in Natural Capital 116
  Policies Aiming at Coordination 119
  Investment in Human Capital 122

Appendix 125

Empirical Approaches to Resource Management
and Environmental Policy: Some Examples 125
  A Case Study of Mangrove Management Options
  in Bintuni Bay, Irian Jaya, Indonesia 125
  A Case Study of the Impact of Pricing of Energy and
  Natural Resources in Spain 130
  Energy and Social Costs and Sectoral Development:
  A Case Study in Agriculture 131
  Costs and Benefits of Environmental Restoration in an
  Urban Squatter Settlement: A Case Study in Rio de Janeiro 137

References 140

The problem of environmental degradation has social roots, and poverty alleviation is a prerequisite for sustainable development. Both poverty and environmental degradation are the result of tendencies inherent in our economic system to externalize environmental and social costs of market transactions – unless adequately checked by social and environmental policies and international agreements. At the same time this externalization tends to enrich particular social groups at the expense of the environment, the population at large and, in particular, disadvantaged social groups who are marginal or external to the decision-making process. Limited access to resources may also leave the poor in situations in which they have limited choices and in which they are more preoccupied with immediate survival needs than in conserving resources for purposes of long-term sustainability. This creates pressure for impoverished groups to exploit increasingly marginal environments to meet immediate survival needs, and leads to environmental degradation and even deeper conditions of poverty in the long run.

This report reviews the literature on the links between poverty and environmental degradation, and elaborates an integrated approach to development. In this approach, a key criterion for sustainable development is whether the needs of the least advantaged and most vulnerable members of society are being met. Other criteria are proposed to cover the issues of efficiency – a traditional concern in economic development – and 'scale' of sustainability. Sustainable development requires that the scale of development be sustainable in bio-physical terms, and that proper balances are made both in terms of intertemporal and intratemporal resource allocation. The scale issue is likely to pose the most difficult policy questions.

Chapter 1 provides a conceptual framework for the remainder of the report. Chapter 2 characterizes the magnitude of the problem and discusses various approaches to measuring the extent and distribution of poverty in relation to environmental degradation. Particular attention is paid to the natural resources upon which poor people depend, and which, properly managed, can provide the basis for sustainable development. Because of the large amount of variability in the conditions of poverty and in its relationship to environmental factors, the report focuses on factors that need to be considered and the kinds of questions that need to be asked, rather than on seeking to provide an extensive description of these variations. Exhaustive compendia of social and economic indicators and of environmental conditions can be found in the reports of the United Nations Development Programme (UNDP), the World Bank, the International Fund for Agricultural Development (IFAD), the United Nations Environment Programme (UNEP), and various non-governmental organizations. The chapter concludes with a discussion of the impacts of environmental degradation on the poor, and institutional constraints that limit the options of the poor for short-term survival strategies.

Chapter 3 reviews a broad range of policies related to poverty and environmental stress based on the criteria of a sustainable scale of resource consumption, equitable distribution and efficient allocation. Public policies are also categorized by the extent of their ramifications; that is, whether their effects are local or global in scope.

This review begins with a discussion of how income distribution affects the values that people place on the environment and illustrates how the market tends to discriminate against the poor because they usually depend directly on natural resources and are forced to sell products at low prices – bringing down the value of environmental resources even when suitable ownership rights have been established. As a result, social movements of the poor to defend access to resources often contribute simultaneously to their conservation and play an important role in internalizing the costs of environmental degradation.

International policies are reviewed to illustrate how they contribute to impoverishment by failing to value natural capital, and to suggest how they can be made more responsive to local needs. International organizations should consider how they might more appropriately participate in assisting local communities to reach objectives that they establish and determine themselves. Legal and property rights structures are discussed to show the relationship between different institutional arrangements and environmental conditions.

Natural resources management policy may benefit from being able to use natural resource accounting (NRA) systems because they can provide the basis for integrated approaches to resource management by identifying environmental costs and benefits, and by illustrating their distribution. Accounts for natural resource depreciation can help to identify linkages between the environment and socio-economic conditions. This issue is of particular relevance to poverty because the poor often depend directly on natural resources. The failure adequately to value natural resources implies a failure adequately to value the extent to which ecosystem services, directly or indirectly, subsidize the economy as well as to value the non-market economic contributions of the poor to society and, often, their intimate understanding of resource variability and sustainable use.

Some case studies that apply these concepts are presented in an Appendix. One case study shows that the poor are disproportionately affected by depletion of natural resources and environmental degradation, because they are generally excluded from the private short-term gains that are derived from such resources. Other case studies show that in addition to protecting agricultural genetic diversity, traditional agro-ecological systems (1) may be more efficient in terms of the amount of food produced in relation to the amount of energy consumed, and (2) absorb more labour and provide a basis for sustaining rural communities. Another case study illustrates the costs and benefits of environmental restoration in urban squatter settlements.

Chapter 3 concludes with a discussion of proposals for integrated resource management strategies, which are based on cooperation among stakeholders, and the development of institutions for collective action.

The conclusions and recommendations set out in Chapter 4 elaborate on some of the implications for public policy and identify actions that could have the most impact and that should receive the highest priority for poverty alleviation in a manner that is consistent with the long-term goals of sustainable development. Some of these are highlighted below:

- The report strongly confirms that development cannot be sustainable unless it meets the needs of the least advantaged members of society.
- Two main policy strategies to pursue are: (1) the use and reinforcement of existing institutions with an expanded range of instruments to facilitate them to contribute to the sustainability of development; and (2) the creation of new institutions at all relevant levels (from local to international) that can address two crucial issues in relation to sustainability: that of scale and that of equity.
- Economic policies primarily use market instruments to achieve allocational efficiency. While these instruments can be useful in that respect, they typically do not address the issues of resource distribution and the scale of consumption; in fact, they may even aggravate conditions in terms of sustainability and scale. Addressing these will require action at all levels – local, regional and global – which can only be achieved through collaboration among all stakeholders and the development of new, more adaptive institutional structures.
- To a substantial degree, failures of the market mechanism to reflect the environmental and resource costs may be corrected by policy interventions (including certain types of tax reforms); wherever such corrections can be made they should be considered by governments as potential policy instruments for ensuring sustainable development. Thus, market forces may be harnessed or mobilized if efficiency, effectiveness and acceptability considerations suggest that this system is preferable to other types of institutional change.

- Strong and socially sustainable institutions for the conservation of natural resources through collective action are a prerequisite for environmental sustainability. This implies that investments are required in both natural and human capital. Improvements in nutrition, education and health can lengthen the time-horizons of the poor, begin to restore communities and provide the political will and institutional capacity needed to protect natural capital.

- Protection of natural capital requires full cost accounting for the depreciation of natural resources, which are often not valued because they are outside the market. Such accounts could then provide the basis for establishing specific policies. It also implies that environmental and resource costs be internalized in commodity prices as the basis for fair trade. One vehicle for this would be a tax on resource consumption rather than on labour and income. This would also provide incentives to reduce material consumption and increase employment. Revenues from such taxes might also provide funds for public investment in natural capital protection, restoration and enhancement.

- Land reform that includes recognition of traditional structures of land tenure and common property rights can also provide the assurances needed by the poor to lengthen their time-horizons and broaden their options for resource management. A common property framework for the management of natural resources, rather than presuming open access to these resources, would recognize poor people as stakeholders and can also provide an equitable institutional framework for resource management.

- Support is needed for ecologically based technologies that require less inputs of fossil fuels and manufactured capital by taking advantage of the self-organizing properties of ecosystems and the assets of the poor, such as their labour and knowledge of their environment, and for the development of institutions for collective action.

- International organizations have an important role to play by establishing a base of common knowledge as a catalyst for social action, enhancing communications between groups, and strengthening community social organizations.

- International organizations could contribute to sustainable development and poverty eradication by explicitly mobilizing structural reforms in that direction, by defining trade policies that would help keep economic processes within environmentally compatible boundaries and, for example, by furthering fair prices which internalize non-market and uncertain environmental and resource factors.

This report arises from a deep concern with the issues of poverty and environmental degradation and their inter-relationships. The concern stems from the observations that (1) poverty and environmental degradation have the same or related root causes, (2) poverty reduction is a prerequisite for sustainable development, and (3) that past attempts to address these issues have mostly suffered from a lack of integration. However, it is fair to say that this is changing, due to a process of adaptation of world views to the realities of the poverty-degradation trap that faces so many people – if not the human species as such. This chapter briefly deals with the phenomena of poverty and environmental degradation and outlines the main dimensions of a more integrated approach towards them.

The Growth of Poverty, Disparity and Environmental Degradation

Poverty, Environment and Development

The protection of the environment and of natural resources is an essential part of development: without adequate environmental capital, development is undermined and this in turn may reduce the resources available for investing in maintaining and enhancing the environmental resource base (World Bank 1992). The poor are both victims and agents of environmental damage, and hence alleviating poverty is not only a moral imperative but also a prerequisite for environmental sustainability and sustainable development (World Bank 1992).

In 1978, Robert McNamara, former president of the World Bank, described absolute poverty as 'a condition of life so limited by malnutrition, illiteracy, disease, squalid surroundings, high infant mortality, and low life expectancy as to be beneath any reasonable definition of human decency.' Poverty, however, is not merely a condition but is the result of a process of impoverishment that may be characterized as a downward spiral that flows from one generation to the next, drawing in increasing numbers of people. From a developmental perspective, the primary task is to eliminate poverty, as is recognized in the Declaration of Rio and Agenda 21. Even though substantial progress has taken place in terms of the average levels of consumption and life expectancy, yet more than one-fifth of humanity lives in acute poverty and the percentage of the population in developing countries below the poverty line is around 30%. Up to 40% of the world population may be defined as poor, if poverty is measured according to whether they have a standard of living that includes adequate food, safe and sufficient supplies of water, secure shelter and access to education and health care (WHO 1992).

The relationship between poverty and environment first emerged as a divisive issue at the United Nations Stockholm Conference on the Human Environment in 1972, where former Indian Prime Minister Indira Gandhi attributed pollution primarily to poverty and underdevelopment. At that conference, developing countries expressed concern that environmental goals could detract from their development goals. *The World Conservation Strategy*, released in 1980 by IUCN – The World Conservation Union, UNEP and WWF – World Wide Fund for Nature, recognized that conservation could not be achieved without alleviating poverty and coined the term 'sustainable development'. These concerns also provided the impetus for the work of the World Commission on Environment and Development, also known as the Brundtland Commission, which recognized the need for the integration of environment and development concerns, and for international equity. The Commission's report, *Our Common Future* (WCED 1987), and its recommendations, provided the basis for the agenda at the 1992 Earth Summit on Environment and Development (UNCED), which was largely a dialogue between the North and South on strategies for moving towards a sustainable future. The UNCED conference recognized both the relationship between poverty and environmental degradation in underdeveloped countries, as well as the problem of unsustainable production and consumption patterns in the developed countries. A concerted effort to alleviate poverty was established as a priority for the 21st century. In the long run all human beings should be capable of mobilizing and developing an adequate and sustainable supply of the means of living (UNCED, Agenda 21).

The Development of Poverty

Here we confine ourselves to a broad overview of how poverty has developed. A more detailed analysis will be presented in Chapter 2. During the 1980s, in spite of an overall increase in economic growth, the numbers of people living in absolute poverty increased from approximately three-quarters of a billion to the current 1.4 billion or one-fourth of humanity (UNDP 1992). Absolute numbers of poor people have increased with growing populations, even though there has been a fall in the percentage of the population below the poverty line. In Africa however, the poor have also increased in proportion to the rest of the population. Largely as a result of high population growth rates in the developing world, the number of people living in poverty is expected to continue to increase unless there are profound changes in the structure of the world economy.

Exceptions are found in some East Asian countries, where there has been a decline in both the absolute numbers of poor and in the percentage of the population that is poor. Although circumstances in individual countries differ, much of the progress in human development in East Asia is based on the redistribution of assets through land reform; investment in health, education, and skill development; and government support for building economic capacity. Land reform efforts in the 1950s in the Republic of Korea, for example, increased the proportion of land owners to tenants, which subsequently increased the labour absorbed per hectare by 4.7% a year. In Taiwan, land reform increased employment in the agricultural sector from 400,000 to 2 million from 1952 to 1968. New crops, multiple-cropping and irrigation with improved water management created even more job opportunities in food processing after the harvest from 11,000 to 144,000. These changes in turn expanded domestic markets for goods and services. East Asian countries also had lower rates of unemployment than OECD countries (UNDP 1993).

The relationship of poverty to environmental degradation is a direct one in developing countries, as their economies rely relatively heavily on extraction of primary commodities. Developed countries also saw an increase in poverty in the 1980s. In the United States for example, the average level of poverty rose from 24,792 or 11.8% in the 1970s, to 32,893 or 13.8% from 1980-91. In 1992, one in five or 14.6 million children (21.9%) were in poverty, up from 11,543 (18.3%) in 1980. Estimates of homelessness range from 228,000 to 600,000 a night, of which 100,000 are children. In addition, 5.5 million children a year experience hunger. Conditions of poverty in developed countries are different from those in undeveloped countries because there is greater access to infrastructure and government assistance programmes. However, even in the United States, poor children are much more likely than non-poor children to die from infections and parasitic disease, from accidents and violence, and from all causes combined. Others suffer needless health and learning problems, abnormally stunted growth, and physical wasting that lead to low test scores and behaviour problems. In both developed and undeveloped countries, poor and low-income people are disproportionately affected by environmental degradation and are more likely to be exposed to toxic pollutants in their homes and workplaces.

Disparity

Between 1960 and 1990, there was also an increase in economic disparity. In 1960, the richest 20% of world population had incomes 30 times greater than the poorest 20%. By 1990, the richest 20% of the population had 60 times more than the poorest 20%, measured *between* countries. If maldistribution *within* countries is included, the income of the richest 20% is 150 times greater than that of the poorest 20%. The poorest 20% receive 0.2% of global commercial bank lending, 1.3% of global investment, 1% of global trade and 1.4% of income. These figures have decreased since 1960. It is expected that this disparity will continue to widen.

Although general indicators of development, such as GNP per capita, life-expectancy at birth, infant mortality and calories per capita, have steadily improved as a result of technological innovations, poverty is growing and the environment is being stressed on larger scales than ever before (Gallopin *et al.* 1989).

Poverty and Environment

Poor people may become trapped into short time-horizons with respect to resources over which they have little or no control because they lack assurances of future access to resources and because they lack other economic opportunities. To the extent that they are excluded from participation in the market economy, they also rely directly on non-marketed natural resources for their immediate survival.

Population growth and landlessness (or near landlessness) create pressure for poor people to exploit increasingly marginal rural and urban environments for survival in the short term, in a manner that leads to resource degradation, which creates more poverty and jeopardizes survival in the long term. These marginal land areas are either remote and ecologically fragile rural areas, or are, increasingly, at the edges of growing urban areas. Ecologically fragile rural areas in developing countries are primarily arid and semi-arid lands, hillsides and tropical forests.

Deforestation in tropical countries, allegedly for the purpose of increasing food production, has instead often decreased it. For example, Haiti has 2% of its forests intact but agricultural production has dropped 15% in the last decade. The correlation between poverty and environmental degradation is particularly acute in Africa, where a map of absolute poverty coincides with areas of deforestation (Leonard 1993). The poorest countries are also located in places where water is either scarce for part of the year or drought occurs in intermittent years, or where high evaporation makes it unavailable for human use (Falkenmark and Lindh 1993). These circumstances also occur in developed countries that have, so far, managed to overcome regional water scarcities through the use of technology, because of their greater access to technical knowledge, energy resources, other inputs and money. Twenty years of land clearing in the Amazon rain forest did not improve the human condition, but led instead to the exponential growth of malaria cases, a high prevalence of trauma, increased child mortality and malnutrition and, in some areas, the endemism of schistosomiasis.

It is estimated that 80% of households in developing countries rely on wood as their primary energy source. One study (CSE 1990), in a village in the central

Himalayas in India, found that less than 6% of hours worked by the villagers was devoted to market activities. Most of this time was devoted to cultivation (30%); fodder collection (20%); fuel collection, animal care, and grazing (24%); and household chores (20%) (Dasgupta 1993). Poor countries in general also rely heavily on exports of natural capital, in the form of primary commodities, which does not contribute to development because the proceeds are primarily used to pay national debts rather than to invest in the development of other forms of capital.

Changing World Views

Since the 1972 Stockholm Conference on the Human Environment, new paradigms have begun to emerge in the economics of both environment and development. International development organizations such as the World Bank and UNDP have begun to recognize that growth in national income does not necessarily lead to improvement in well-being, and have adopted a new development agenda that includes a focus on human needs and poverty alleviation in addition to economic growth. According to UNDP, economic growth is a means to the goal of human development. Human development is concerned with both growth and distribution, and is defined as the process of enlarging people's choices, increasing opportunities, ranging from the physical environment to economic and political freedoms, and the development of human capabilities, and productive use, in order to contribute to GNP growth and employment for the purpose of achieving long-term social goals. Participatory approaches are required to determine human needs and long-term social goals, as well as how they might best be achieved (UNDP, 1992).

There is also increased recognition that natural capital is a scarce and limiting factor rather than a free good, and that new socially and ecologically based methods of economic analysis are needed that account for the depreciation of natural as well as human capital. Until recently, the language of the mainstream in economics has defined the economy mainly in market terms, without giving much attention to non-market elements such as subsidies provided by ecosystem services, subsistence activities, household labour or cultural aspects of human social systems. Manufactured capital and technical progress are considered to be substitutes rather than complements to natural and human capital (e.g. Solow 1992). Conventional economics has focused on allocative efficiency, giving little weight to distributive justice and even less to sustainability (Opschoor 1992). Furthermore, there has been increasing recognition of the fact that many of the poor are excluded from or are peripheral to the market system precisely because they rely more heavily on natural resources often inadequately priced and the informal economy. This has to be translated in systematic ways to take into account such 'non-market' aspects of the economy and the services rendered by natural capital.

In the past, natural capital has been treated as superabundant and priced at zero, so it did not really matter whether it was a complement or a substitute for man-made capital. Now, remaining natural capital appears to be both scarce and complementary, and therefore limiting. For example, the fish catch is limited not by the number of fishing boats, but by the remaining populations of fish in the sea. Cut timber is limited not by the number of sawmills, but by the remaining standing forests. Pumped crude oil is limited not by man-made pumping capacity, but by remaining stocks of petroleum in the ground. The natural capital of the atmosphere's capacity to serve as a sink for CO_2 is likely to be even more limiting to the rate at which petroleum can be burned than is the source limit of the remaining oil in the ground (Daly, 1994).

In spite of the dependence of poor countries on their natural resources such as soil and its cover, water, forests, animals and fisheries, environmental resources make but perfunctory appearances in government planning models, and they are often ignored in most development economics (Dasgupta 1993). Previously, development was viewed as merely a problem of modernizing traditional societies, and developing countries were expected to follow the same development path as the developed countries regardless of differences in resource availability, social structure, political orientation, historical background and colonial heritage (IFAD 1992). In the 1960s and 1970s, an inward strategy of development was pursued in which developing countries tried to industrialize for a regional export market with financing from their agricultural sector and high trade barriers on imports. It did not work because they did not have the technical knowledge to compete with multinational corporations and had to lower trade barriers in order to import needed raw materials. From the 1980s onward, development was pursued by following and promoting a strategy of export-oriented economic growth based on trade liberalization, and currency devaluation, as is reflected in the World Bank's and IMF's structural adjustment programmes. This approach failed to recognize local circumstances, the potential for internally generated growth, and the contributions of traditional institutions and knowledge. It was not inherently geared towards sustainability, as it relied on external circumstances over which developing countries have no control (such as commodity prices) and neglected agro-ecological systems that were adapted to local environments. In some countries poverty persisted or worsened in spite of a strong growth of GDP. New agricultural technologies such as improved seed, chemical fertilizers, and irrigation did increase production of basic crops and averted mass starvation in spite of a population increase of over 2 billion people from 1960 to 1990. However, they also contributed to environmental degradation in the long run, and did not contribute to self-reliance, which could have generated internal momentum for sustainability. More recent documents by the World Bank reflect a commitment to so-called 'weak sustainability': maintaining the level of accumulated capital, including human and environmental capital, so that if there is a loss of natural capital this would be more than compensated by capital increases elsewhere (World Bank 1992).

Our economic system reflects human interactions with the environment and our values as a society. The conventional view of the economy as being regulated by the 'hidden hand' of the market, which linked the individual pursuit of well-being and greed to the common good, failed to recognize the pervasiveness of social and ecological externalities that leads to huge differences between individual and community interests. It has been suggested that this unrestricted maximization of individual interests in the presence of these externalities can only lead to an unsustainable society, and perhaps chaos. Poverty can then be seen as a social condition of chronic insecurity resulting from the breakdown of economic, demographic, ecological, cultural and social systems, and causing groups of people to lose the capacity to adapt and to survive. It is analogous to environmental degradation, which may be defined as the loss of resilience and capacity for self-renewal in ecosystems, of which human beings are a part.

In new and more integrated approaches to development, the importance of social and ecological externalities and the need for community investment in human, cultural and natural capital are recognized as prerequisites for sustainable development. Such approaches also go beyond a static equilibrium view of the economy and towards the study of the economy as a dynamic system in the context of the ecosystem upon which it depends. They focus on human needs because those needs drive interactions between humans and the environment, the understanding of which is fundamental to resolving the problem of sustainability. One such new approach is called 'ecological economics', which broadens traditional economic as well as ecological approaches by also drawing on contributions from such other disciplines relevant to the problem of sustainability as anthropology, sociology and the study of institutions for the management of common property resources as well as other areas of the natural sciences relevant to the understanding of ecosystem processes.

From an ecological and an economic perspective, both poverty and environmental degradation are symptoms of a poorly functioning economic system. Ignoring the huge social and ecological externalities that exist provides incentives to lower prices at the expense of human and natural capital, leading to poor working conditions, low wages and environmental degradation. Inequalities of wealth and power contribute to environmental degradation because they permit some people to reap the market benefits while others pay the non-market costs.

In addition to inequitable distribution, the causes of poverty and environmental degradation may be traced to problems related to the sustainability of the scale of resource consumption and environmental pressure, and the efficiency of the allocation of resources. Among many other things, development means increases in the level of economic activities. These activities take place within environmental constraints that follow from the need to maintain the productivity of biospheric processes at certain desired levels; they have to stay within the 'space' that the biosphere allows for utilization by societies (Opschoor 1992). Economic development can only remain within this environmental utilization space if it leads to a 'delinking' of economic growth and claims on the environment (World Bank 1992). Otherwise, the scale of economic activity will eventually exceed the environmental space, with as a consequence a declining environmental capital base which may threaten the future potential for maintaining and enhancing per capita consumption.

Putting these broader perspectives into practice will require sets of indicators that reflect the relationships between ecological and economic systems. Ideally, indicators of sustainable development should provide information that reflects the scale of the human economy relative to the broader ecosystem or natural capital that is necessary to support human needs, and should integrate data about environmental degradation with data that illustrates how environmental costs and benefits are distributed among diverse social groups. If possible, indicators should also provide information that can be used to project trends, to model the links between economic activity and ecosystem health to demonstrate cause and effect relationships, and allow for sensitivity analyses to deal with uncertainty (Kuik, Onno and Verbruggen 1991, OECD 1993, Bartelmus 1994, Bakkes *et al.* 1994, Weterings and Opschoor 1994).

Finally, some developments in the global political economy should be mentioned here, as they set the scene for, and influence current thinking on, economic development: the growing trend towards globalization and the recent change in the economic system in the formerly socialist countries of Central and Eastern Europe.

The trend towards globalization of the world economy is manifest in increases in the volume of international trade and of international financial transactions. Trade liberalization and the opening up of new markets appear to go hand in hand. The benefits of these processes are spread unevenly both in a geographical sense and in terms of income distribution. It appears that a number of poor countries and even a large proportion of the poor in several newly industrializing countries remain at the periphery of these processes. Apart from these distributional concerns, there may be other ones. Globalization effectively means the spreading of a rather uniform but luxurious lifestyle; amongst the long-term consequences of this are a reduced cultural diversity and the threats of more widespread unsustainable patterns of consumption.

The economies of the countries in Central and Eastern Europe are now in transition towards becoming market economies. This has had several repercussions worth mentioning in the context of poverty and environment. One obvious one has been the increased efforts by industrialized countries to boost development in the economies in transition, possibly competing for attention with development needs elsewhere in the world. Another repercussion, and one that has influenced views on development strategies, has been the increasing tendency to rely on market forces to shape and orient the development process. From an environmental point of view the latter position must be regarded as one that merits concern, as market forces themselves do not automatically orient themselves on sustainability criteria and do not adequately address environmental market failures. Yet, it is important to take this tendency into account and to translate it into appropriate as well as acceptable instruments and mechanisms for environmental policies and resource management.

2 WORLD POVERTY AND ENVIRONMENTAL DEGRADATION

In this chapter the nature and extent of both the poverty problem and the environmental problem are discussed. The relationship between the two should be clear: the poor especially depend directly on natural resources and, in so far as the maintenance of these resources requires outlays and even investments, the poor are least equipped to carry these out. These inter-relationships are given special attention. Institutional aspects of the causes of poverty and unsustainability, as well as possible ways out of the social and environmental trap in which the poor typically find themselves, are dealt with.

The Nature and Extent of World Poverty

Poverty may be absolute or relative and may be defined in various ways. The condition of *absolute poverty* generally refers to people whose income is insufficient to obtain the minimum necessities for purely physical efficiency. There is no definitive measure because nutritional needs and other minimal necessities vary according to climate, age, sex and health. Often the measurement is based on the percentage of income required for food and housing needs. The 'poverty line' as defined by the World Bank is about $420 per capita, in 1990 prices (World Bank 1992). *Relative poverty* is defined by the ability to live according to cultural norms and expectations or contemporary standards of living measured according to the median income of the society in which it occurs.

The most widely used indicators of development are GNP and per capita income, which provide an aggregate measure of market-based production and consumption, and the degree of access to productive and consumptive goods. With respect to poverty, they are used to develop a headcount of persons below the poverty line. However, as the international development organizations have shifted their development goals away from an exclusive focus on economic growth and towards poverty alleviation and human needs, they have also begun to consider the distribution of income below the poverty line, and to supplement these measures with a broader spectrum of social and environmental indicators such as health and educational attainment. Access to health and education services depends more on the extent to which these are provided by governments than on the incomes of individuals (Dasgupta 1993). Although indicators are useful for developing a broad social profile, local case studies are needed to characterize the circumstances of individual communities and their relationship to resources if sustainable development efforts are to be successful. The following section provides an overview of poverty indicators and characterizes different conditions of poverty to illustrate the variability of its relationship to the use of natural resources and environmental degradation.

Measurement of Poverty

Approaches used by UNDP

UNDP has developed a Human Development Index (HDI), based on a definition of human development as the process of increasing people's choices, focusing on both the formation of human capabilities and on the use of those capabilities. The HDI ranks countries according to their progress towards the maximum attainable values for life expectancy, educational attainment and (weighted) income indicators. These factors are combined to provide a composite of diverse data. It is assumed that nutritional status and child mortality are reflected in life expectancy, and that employment rates are reflected in real income. The regular HDI does not reveal disparities among different social, economic or regional groups, although a separate HDI was calculated for 33 countries for which data was available, based on gender, income and regional differences, to illustrate disparities within countries. India as a whole, for example, ranks 121, while its most populous state, Uttar Pradesh, ranks 147. Male and female disparities are widest in the developing countries. In Canada for example, the female HDI is 86% of the male HDI, in Costa Rica it is two-thirds, and in Kenya it is one half.

There is little relationship between a country's GNP and HDI rank or between income and human development. In a comparison of five countries with a similar GNP per capita, UNDP found wide disparities in social welfare. For example, Guyana, Kenya, Ghana, Pakistan and Haiti all have a GNP per capita of approximately $380. Among them, Guyana has the highest HDI rank (105), and Haiti the lowest (137). Pakistan has an infant mortality rate twice that of Guyana and an illiteracy rate three times higher. Some countries have an HDI rank that is way ahead of per capita income rank, while others have a per capita income rank that is higher than their HDI rank (see Table 1). On the other hand, human development factors, such as improvements in nutrition and health, have sometimes been shown to account for significant per capita income growth.

HDI does not directly absorb or reflect information on environmental conditions or the sustainability of the societies for which it is calculated. Life expectancy may reflect environmental conditions in a broad sense, but does not capture specific

TABLE 1

Comparison of HDI with GNP per capita Rank

	HDI 1990	GNP per capita (US$) 1990	GNP Rank
Japan	0.983	25840	3
Canada	0.982	20380	11
Norway	0.979	22830	6
Switzerland	0.978	32250	1
Sweden	0.977	23780	5
USA	0.976	21810	10
Australia	0.972	16560	18
France	0.971	19590	13
Netherlands	0.97	17570	16
United Kingdom	0.964	16080	19
Iceland	0.96	22090	9
Germany	0.957	22360	8
Denmark	0.955	22440	7
Finland	0.954	24540	4
Austria	0.952	19000	14
Belgium	0.952	17580	15
New Zealand	0.947	12570	21
Luxembourg	0.943	29010	2
Israel	0.938	11160	25
Barbados	0.928	6480	32
Ireland	0.925	10370	27
Italy	0.924	16880	17
Spain	0.923	11010	26
Hong Kong	0.913	11700	22
Greece	0.902	6010	33
Czechoslovakia	0.892	3190	46
Cyprus	0.89	8230	28
Hungary	0.887	2780	49
Lithuania	0.881	3110	47
Uruguay	0.881	2620	51
Trinidad and Tobago	0.877	3460	43
Bahamas	0.875	11550	23
Korea, Rep. of	0.872	5450	35
Estonia	0.872	4170	39
Latvia	0.868	3590	40
Chile	0.864	1950	71
Russian Federation	0.862	3430	44
Belarus	0.861	3110	48
Malta	0.855	6680	31
Bulgaria	0.854	2320	64
Portugal	0.853	4950	36
Costa Rica	0.852	1900	72
Singapore	0.849	11200	24
Brunei Darussalam	0.847	–	
Ukraine	0.844	2500	55
Argentina	0.832	2380	59
Armenia	0.831	2380	60
Poland	0.831	1690	76

	HDI 1990	GNP per capita (US$) 1990	GNP Rank
Georgia	0.829	2120	69
Venezuela	0.824	2560	53
Dominica	0.819	2220	67
Kuwait	0.815	–	
Kazakhstan	0.805	2600	52
Mexico	0.805	2490	56
Qatar	0.802	15870	20
Mauritius	0.794	2310	65
Bahrain	0.79	6830	30
Malaysia	0.79	2330	82
Grenada	0.787	2130	68
Antigua and Barbuda	0.785	4290	38
Azerbaijan	0.77	1640	78
Colombia	0.77	1260	87
Seychelles	0.761	4820	37
Moldova, Rep. of	0.758	2390	58
Suriname	0.751	3350	45
Turkmenistan	0.746	1690	77
United Arab Emirates	0.738	19870	12
Panama	0.738	1900	73
Jamaica	0.736	1500	82
Brazil	0.73	2680	50
Fiji	0.73	1780	74
Saint Lucia	0.72	2350	61
Turkey	0.717	1640	79
Thailand	0.715	1420	84
Cuba	0.711	–	
Saint Vincent	0.709	1710	75
Romania	0.709	1620	80
Albania	0.699	–	
Saint Kits and Nevis	0.697	3540	42
Uzbekistan	0.695	1340	85
Syrian Arab Rep.	0.694	1000	94
Belize	0.689	1960	70
Kyrgyzstan	0.689	1570	81
Saudi Arabia	0.688	7070	29
South Africa	0.673	2530	54
Sri Lanka	0.663	470	118
Libyan Arab Jamahiriya	0.658	–	
Tajikistan	0.657	1130	88
Ecuador	0.646	960	98
Paraguay	0.641	1090	91
Korea, Dem. Rep. of	0.64	–	
Philippines	0.603	730	105
Tunisia	0.6	1450	83
Oman	0.598	5650	34
Peru	0.592	1100	89
Iraq	0.589	–	
Samoa	0.586	920	100
Dominican Rep.	0.586	830	103
Mongolia	0.578	–	
China	0.566	370	130
Lebanon	0.565	–	

	HDI 1990	GNP per capita (US$) 1990	GNP Rank
Iran, Islamic Rep. of	0.557	2490	57
Botswana	0.552	2230	66
Guyana	0.541	380	129
Vanuatu	0.533	1100	90
Algeria	0.528	2330	63
Indonesia	0.515	560	113
Gabon	0.503	3550	41
El Salvador	0.503	1000	95
Nicaragua	0.5	420	121
Maldives	0.497	450	119
Guatemala	0.489	910	101
Cape Verde	0.479	680	107
Honduras	0.472	640	109
Viet Nam	0.472	–	
Swaziland	0.458	1030	93
Solomon Islands	0.439	590	112
Morocco	0.433	970	97
Lesotho	0.431	540	114
Zimbabwe	0.398	650	108
Bolivia	0.398	630	110
Myanmar	0.39	–	
Egypt	0.389	610	111
São Tome and Principe	0.374	400	124
Congo	0.372	1000	96
Kenya	0.369	370	131
Madagascar	0.327	230	143
Papua New Guinea	0.318	850	102
Zambia	0.314	420	122
Pakistan	0.311	400	125
Ghana	0.311	390	127
Cameroon	0.31	960	99
India	0.309	360	133
Namibia	0.289	1080	92
Cote d'Ivoire	0.286	750	104
Haiti	0.275	370	132
Tanzania, U. Rep. of	0.27	110	157
Comoros	0.269	480	117
Zaire	0.262	220	144
Nigeria	0.246	290	140
Lao People's Dem. Rep.	0.246	200	147
Yemen	0.233	540	115
Liberia	0.222	–	
Togo	0.218	410	123
Uganda	0.194	180	150
Bangladesh	0.189	210	145
Rwanda	0.186	310	138
Cambodia	0.186	170	154
Senegal	0.182	710	106
Ethiopia	0.172	120	155
Nepal	0.17	180	151
Malawi	0.168	200	146
Burundi	0.167	210	146
Equatorial Guinea	0.164	340	135

	HDI 1990	GNP per capita (US$) 1990	GNP Rank
Central African Rep.	0.159	390	128
Mozambique	0.154	80	158
Sudan	0.152	400	126
Bhutan	0.15	190	149
Angola	0.143	–	
Mauritania	0.14	500	116
Benin	0.113	360	134
Djibouti	0.104	–	
Guinea-Bissau	0.09	180	152
Chad	0.088	180	153
Somalia	0.087	120	156
Gambia	0.086	340	136
Mali	0.082	280	141
Niger	0.08	310	139
Burkina Faso	0.074	330	137
Afghanistan	0.066		
Sierra Leone	0.065	250	142
Jordan	0.0582	1340	86
Guinea	0.045	440	120

Source: UNDP 1993.

environmental quality aspects, certainly not in a prospective sense. And the income variable will not capture environmental change either, as the GDP statistic from which it is derived does not measure the depreciation of natural capital or environmental quality. This depreciation is particularly significant for developing countries that rely heavily on the primary economic sector. Depreciation of forests, soils and livestock amounted to 6% of Costa Rica's GDP from 1970 to 1990, and 9% of Indonesia's in terms of forests, soils and fisheries (Repetto *et al.* 1989, Repetto 1991).

Approaches used by the World Bank

The framework for poverty analyses used by the World Bank measures poverty based on the income or expenditure level that can sustain a bare minimum standard of living based on caloric intake. They acknowledge, however, that this standard is difficult to define because household income and per capita expenditures do not include non-market factors such as household subsistence production, which may be significant among the poor. Although individual country profiles may differ, for purposes of inter-country comparisons, people are considered to fall below the line for absolute poverty if their income is under US$370 per capita (1985 prices), and are considered extremely poor if their income is under $275 (in PPP, purchasing power parity). A higher figure is used for the urban poverty line because the relationship between caloric intake and expenditure level is higher in urban than in rural areas. A 'poverty gap index' is then used to determine distribution below the poverty line. This index consists of the difference between the poverty line and the mean income of the poor expressed as a ratio of the poverty line (also known as the 'income gap ratio'). Measures of income and consumption are supplemented by nutrition, under-five mortality and school enrollment rates. Based on 1985 data, the World Bank estimates that one-third of the population of the developing world is below the upper poverty line, and 18% are below the lower poverty line (see Table 2).

TABLE 2

Numbers of Poor People in the Developing Countries during 1985

	Extremely poor			Poor (including extremely poor)			Social indicators		
	Number (millions)	Headcount index (%)	Poverty Gap	Number (millions)	Headcount index (%)	Poverty Gap	Under-5 mortality (per thousand)	Life expectancy (years)	Net primary enrollment rate (%)
Sub-Saharan Africa	120	30	4	180	47	11	196	50	56
East Asia	120	9	0.4	280	20	1	96	67	96
China	80	8	1	210	20	3	58	69	93
South Asia	300	29	3	520	51	10	172	56	74
India	250	33	4	420	55	12	199	57	81
Eastern Europe	3	4	0.2	6	8	0.5	23	71	90
Middle East and North Africa	40	21	1	60	31	2	148	61	75
Latin America and the Caribbean	50	12	1	70	19	1	5	66	92
All developing countries	633	18	1	1116	33	3	121	62	83

Note: The poverty line in 1985 PPP is $275 per capita a year for the extremely poor and $370 per capita a year for the poor. The headcount index is defined as the percentage of the population below the poverty line. The 95% confidence interval around the point estimates for the headcount indices are Sub-Saharan Africa, 19, 76; East Asia, 21, 22; South Asia, 50, 33; Eastern Europe, 7, 10; Middle East and North Africa, 13, 51; Latin America and the caribbean, 14, 30; and all developing countries, 28, 39.

The poverty gap is defined as the aggregate income shortfall of the poor as a percentage of aggregate consumption. Under-5 mortality rates are for 1980-85, except for China and South Asia, where the period is 1975-80.

Source: United Nations and World Bank data 1989.

A more detailed poverty profile for individual countries may also include short-term income indicators, such as rural terms of trade, unskilled wage rates, household income and expenditures and a lower consumer price index that is weighted toward food and fuel consumption in order better to reflect the consumption patterns of the poor. Social indicators may include the share of public expenditures for basic social services in GDP, rates for net primary school enrollment, under-five mortality, immunization, child malnutrition, female-to-male life expectancy, total fertility, maternal mortality, female and adult literacy and the accumulation and maintenance of assets by the poor. Here, as with UNDP, the conclusion is that the World Bank approach to the measurement of poverty does not embrace the environmental aspects directly, and hardly indirectly.

Approaches used by IFAD

The International Fund for Agricultural Development (IFAD) (1992) has characterized poverty in rural areas using four macro- level indices that measure food security, the depth of poverty, the extent to which basic needs are being met and relative welfare, which consists of an average of the first three indices. These indices illustrate a general decline in food security between the mid-1960s and mid-1980s (see Table 3), particularly in sub-Saharan Africa, and increasing severity of poverty. Inconsistency in the relationship between GNP per capita and the extent to which basic needs are being met, demonstrates the importance of considering how budget resources are allocated and the cost-effectiveness of the delivery of services. The 20 lowest ranking countries on the combined index of relative welfare were also consistent with those considered the most vulnerable based on the HDI ranking method of UNDP.

At the household level, the primary consideration is the ability to meet minimum consumption needs during periods of economic difficulty and calamity. Poverty at the household level is characterized by the extent of material deprivation, isolation, alienation, dominance and dependence, lack of participation and freedom of choice, lack of assets, vulnerability and insecurity. In addition to providing some measure of the quality of life, these factors serve to illustrate some of the social conditions that prevent an escape from poverty. For example, isolation from roads and mass communications because of illiteracy and geographical location cuts off information access, marginalizes people from the political process and affects income through inability to market agricultural production. Dependence leads to unequal social relations because it depresses bargaining power, forcing farmers to sell commodities at low prices and to accept unfavourable terms of agreement in sharecropping. In South Asia, for example, in exchange for the use of land, a sharecropper might be required to pay for up to 100% of inputs and provide all of the labour in exchange for 35% to 50% of the output. Because of these factors, the poor are also the most vulnerable to risk and the least able to adapt to changing conditions resulting from calamities such as drought and famine, natural disasters, social conflicts and illness. External shocks, such as the collapse of commodity prices, may force poor people to sell their assets and cause further price collapse.

Because of fluctuating conditions, IFAD also considers people who are vulnerable. In addition to the absolute poor, this group includes those people who are marginally above the line, are unstable and who move in and out of the poverty group.

TABLE 3

Number of Food Deficit Countries by Region, 1965-67 and 1986-88

Region	1965-67	1986-88
Asia	19	19
Sub-Saharan Africa	28	41
Near East and North Africa	11	12
Latin America and the Caribbean	26	27
Total	84	99
Least developed countries	27	38

Note: Food deficit countries are those with a self-sufficient ratio less than 100.
Source: IFAD 1992.

Types, Locations and a Broad Socio-economic Profile of the Poor

Chapter 1 presented a picture of how poverty has developed over the past years in various parts of the world. In this section the aim is to provide a more detailed analysis, by sketching a socio-economic poverty profile. The majority of the poor (80%) live in rural areas and the numbers of rural poor have increased by 40% over the last two decades despite 40 years of international development assistance. The number of poor in urban areas, currently over 130 million, is increasing even faster – squatter settlements are estimated to be increasing their population at approximately 7% a year compared to 3.5% for urban areas as a whole and 2.1% annually for developing countries in general. By the turn of the century, it is expected that most of the poor population will be urban. These squatter settlements normally lack urban infrastructure and access to basic water and sanitation services. Poverty disproportionately affects particular social groups including women, households headed by women, children and indigenous populations. In the last 20 years, the number of rural women in poverty rose by 50% from 370 million to 565 million compared to 30% for men. More than 250,000 children die of malnutrition and related disease each week. Children in sub-Saharan Africa, of which over 40% are malnourished, have the highest infant mortality rate in the world (180 per 1000), which continues to increase.

Indigenous peoples are another group at more than average risk. In Bolivia, where the overall poverty rate is over 50%, almost three-quarters of the monolingual indigenous population are poor and two-thirds of the bilingual population are poor. In Guatemala, where over 60% of the population is indigenous, only 150 out of 25,000 students in higher education are from the indigenous groups. Even in developed countries, the conditions of indigenous populations sometimes resembles those in developing countries. For example, in Canada, infant mortality among indigenous people is twice the national average; in New Zealand, they are 7 times more likely to be unemployed; and in Australia, they have a 20-year lower life expectancy and are 14 times more likely to be imprisoned.

The majority of those in absolute poverty are clustered in South Asia and sub-Saharan Africa. Post-1988 data indicate that 939 million of those below nationally defined absolute poverty lines reside in rural areas, including 633 million in Asia, 204 million in sub-Saharan Africa, 76 million in Latin America and the Caribbean, and the remainder reside in the Near East and in North Africa. It is also estimated that 80% of the poor people in Latin America live in marginal land areas; the figures for Asia and Africa are 60% and 50%. Table 4 shows a comparison between the share of global population and the share of global GNP in industrial and less-developed countries and the differences between 1960 and 1989.

TABLE 4

Widening Economic Gaps between Regions (% of global figures)

	Global population		Global GNP	
	1960	1989	1960	1989
Sub-Saharan Africa	7.1	9.5	1.9	1.2
South Asia	19.8	22.7	3.1	2.8
East and Southeast Asia (excl. China)	8.8	9.9	1.7	2.9
China	21.8	21.6	3	2
Arab States	3.9	5	1.5	2.5
Latin America and the Caribbean	7.1	8.4	4.7	4.4
Developing countries	68.5	77.1	15.9	15.8
Least developed	6.8	8.4	1	0.5
Industrial countries	31.5	22.9	84.1	84.2

Source: UNDP 1992.

Strategies

The profile presented above suggests that it is important to distinguish different types of poverty because environmental effects, as well as strategies and technical options for poverty alleviation, vary widely depending on whether the poor are located in marginal or resource-rich areas, what their skills are and on what degree of access they have to resources and infrastructure. For example, it may be difficult to alleviate interstitial poverty, which exists where the landless poor reside in resource-rich areas amidst power and affluence, because benefits may be easily preempted by the non-poor. Survival strategies of different groups may range from diversification or intensification of farming, a combination of farm and non-farm employment, permanent or temporary migration, mutual assistance within kinship groups or some combination of these (FAO 1993). Strategies will also depend on factors such as gender, and whether the poor are smallholders, landless pastoralists or fishermen, displaced refugees, in urban areas, or members of indigenous ethnic groups (FAO 1993).

Smallholders, defined as those who own 3 hectares of land or less, comprise 52% of the rural population. As will be discussed in this report, the growth of smallholder productivity is an important strategy for poverty alleviation because this group contributes significantly to the production of traditional crops in a labour-intensive manner. In addition to providing greater employment than large-scale mechanized agriculture that is geared towards the production of export crops, smallholders contribute to subsistence needs and may provide the basis for stable and sustainable rural communities.

Smallholders are at the greatest risk of becoming landless as a result of a large number of factors: population pressure, privatization, illegal land transfers and encroachment by private individuals on common property resources, timber concessions and government development schemes, degradation of environmental and agrarian structures through displacement by large entrepreneurs and mechanization in areas of export crops, collapse of commodity prices, loss of land through indebtedness, natural disasters, absence of safety nets and loss of animal herds in droughts. The landless poor comprise 24% of the rural population, are primarily found in Asia, and also include small artisans and tradesmen. Other sources estimate the landless, together with the near-landless, to comprise almost 60% of rural households in Asia, Africa, and Latin America. Their level of poverty depends on the extent of non-agricultural employment that is available.

Nomadic pastoralists are hard to reach in poverty alleviation efforts because they are mobile and dispersed. Also, the construction of watering points, and the fodder and dry feed supply, for example, are not financed by credit institutions.

They comprise 6% of rural populations and are concentrated in sub-Saharan Africa, North Africa and the Near East.

Indigenous groups are those whose ancestors were the original inhabitants of lands with which they have maintained a strong, fundamental relationship for much longer than the nation-states in which they live. Approximately 6,000 indigenous communities remain (out of 15,000 that are known) based on distinct language classifications, and are found in all parts of the world including developed and developing countries. These groups include approximately 600 million individuals or 10-15% of the world population and have claims to significant amounts of land. Their lands are often expropriated by states because they contain significant natural resources, have sometimes become overflow areas for population pressures, and are increasingly sought after by settlers, loggers and miners and for building dams. The groups face special obstacles to recognition of their land rights because of assimilation policies that fail to recognize their rights as a group and the collective ownership of land and resources. Often governments deny their existence, and they may be displaced with little if any compensation as a result of land privatization, deforestation and such development projects as large dams. They are a particularly significant presence in Botswana, India, Bolivia, Ecuador, Guatemala, Mexico and Peru, although they are located in more than 70 countries. A key consideration for them is the protection of access to their resources and the improvement of living conditions in a manner that is consistent with their cultural heritage.

Refugees and displaced populations comprise 6% of the global population and are rapidly increasing in Africa because of food shortages and armed conflicts. Returning migrants (for example Ghanaians who worked in Nigeria and returned to Ghana at the end of the oil boom) may also resemble displaced populations.

Poverty disproportionately affects women because they are paid less (if at all), have less access to credit, in many cases may not hold title to land, and may have responsibilities for growing food crops and tending livestock in addition to household chores and raising dependent children. Most of their work is outside of the market economy and is neither compensated nor accounted for in national income accounts. This category comprises one-third of rural households in sub-Saharan Africa. Landless households headed by women are the most vulnerable. There are approximately 564 million women below the poverty line, of which 76 million are heads of households and are responsible for the food security of 377 million household members, most of whom are children. These households comprise 12% of rural populations in developing countries, and 16 million of them are landless. In the last 20 years, the number of rural women in poverty rose by 50% (from 370 to 564 million) compared to 30% for men (see Table 5).

TABLE 5

Profile of the Rural Poor in Developing Countries (% of rural population)

	Smallholder farmer population	Landless population	Nomadic pastoralist population	Ethnic indigenous population	Small and artisanal fishermen population	Internally displaced refugee population	Households headed by women as % of rural households 1988
Asia	49	26	2	4.5	4	5	9
Asia (excl. China and India)	51	20	2	2.4	7	5	14
Sub-Saharan Africa	73	11	13	0.9	3	6	31
Near East and North Africa	42	23	5	NA	2	13	17
Latin America	38	31	NA	27.1	5	1	17
The Caribbean	52	24	6	7.3	4	6	12
Least developed countries	67	18	16	1.1	5	7	23

NA: Not available
Source: IFAD 1992.

For a detailed breakdown of rural poverty, its types and its location for each of 56 developing countries, see IFAD (1992). Measurements and indicators only provide general information about a country's social and economic stratification, but local circumstances have to be identified and considered on a case-by-case basis if sustainable development strategies are to be responsive to human needs. After villages with limited resources and inadequate production services have been identified, a household-level analysis is needed. In China for example, in the pastures of Mongolia, IFAD (1992) divided rural dwellers into strata based on sources of income, access to irrigation, grain self-sufficiency, availability of surplus grain for livestock, ownership of livestock, ownership of fruit trees and off-farm employment.

The Nature and Extent of Environmental Degradation

Environmental degradation can be of several types. Roughly speaking, distinctions may be between (1) environmental problems related to the degradation of land and natural resources, and (2) degradation linked to pollution. While the first has been the primary concern in developing countries and the latter in industrialized countries, industrialization in a number of developing countries has tended to blur somewhat this distinction in terms of primary concerns. Yet it remains useful to distinguish resource-related concerns from pollution-related ones and to recognize the significance of resource-related problems, especially in many developing countries. Moreover, in the new global context, a spatial distinction between the North and the South is becoming less and less relevant. Some sectors and regions in some developing countries are as responsible for bringing about the imbalance between different parts of the system as the countries of the 'North'.

This section attempts to illustrate general associations between poverty and environmental conditions by looking at land degradation and the environmental aspects of urbanization. Special attention will be given to the impacts of environmental degradation on the poor and to institutional aspects of the link between poverty and environmental degradation. This section first discusses poverty-environment-population linkages in more general terms.

Poverty-Environment-Population Linkages

The currently accepted paradigm is that levels of population, of consumption patterns and the nature of technology are the three major factors which determine the effect of development on the environment. Although no simple correlations can be established between population and environmental transformations, there is little doubt that the recent extremely rapid increase and the projected further increase in the population of the species *Homo sapiens* on our planet is a major factor affecting global resource use which, together with technology and consumption patterns, contributes to the stress put on the natural environment. To determine carrying capacity – or sustainable patterns of resource use and population levels – we need to understand the interactions of population and per capita resource consumption as mediated by technology, culture, and values (see, e.g., Arizpe *et al.* (1991) for trends in population growth and distribution, and differences in consumption patterns among different sectors of the population).

Each level of resources, when associated with a structure of property rights and a level of technology, is able to provide sustenance to a certain level of population. The emergence of the poverty-resource-degradation trap is the consequence of one of the following scenarios:

(a) a breakdown of property rights institutions,
(b) an over-consumption in one part of the system that reduces the level of consumption that can be sustained by the resource-institution-technology combination,
(c) the failure of technology to evolve in line with increasing demands for waste absorption and for decreased dependence on exhaustible fossil fuel based processes,

(d) an inordinate increase in population in a part of or in the entire system.

Below, we shall proceed by discussing population issues and carrying capacity; this is by way of illustration and is not intended to suggest that population is the major driving force (as is clear from (a) to (d) above).

Population Growth and Distribution

World population has more than doubled since 1950, from 2.5 to 5.4 billion. It is currently growing at the rate of 1.7% a year, and is expected to double again in 40 years. This unprecedented growth in the number of humans has been brought about by a decrease in death rates while birth rates have remained at their traditional high levels or, in some instances, have increased slightly due to better maternal health conditions. In Europe and North America significant mortality declines were already occurring during the second half of the 19th century, mostly due to improved sanitary conditions and food security. Since then life expectancy has steadily increased in the more developed world. On a global scale the most significant change in mortality came in today's less developed countries after World War II, with a generally very successful fight against infectious diseases. More recently rates of mortality improvement have declined because the easy measures had already been taken, and those requiring infrastructural or behavioural changes proved to be much more difficult (Arizpe *et al.* 1991).

On the fertility side, birth rates entered a secular decline in Europe and North America during the first decades of this century. This led to a reduction in the growth rate of the population. The phenomenon of birth rates following the decline of death rates (with some lag) has been described by the notion of demographic transition. While in the more developed regions this transition is essentially completed today, in most less developed countries it is still under way; in some regions – especially Africa – the fertility transition has hardly started.

Any reduction of population growth, even at a level two or three times today's world population, is expected to result in extreme aging of the population. In addition to influencing the momentum of population growth, a society's age distribution has a significant impact on consumption patterns, the value system and even culture. The age structure of the population also has implications for economic structure and dependency burdens, ranging from educational expenses for the young to health care and other support for the elderly. Only further exponential growth will keep the population young.

The distribution of the population of the major regions of the world has changed significantly over the past years and is likely to change even more in the future. In 1950 one-third of the world population lived in the developed world. In 2000 this fraction will have declined to about one-fifth, despite the fact that the population of the developed countries grew by about 50%.

During the second half of our century the population of Africa has quadrupled from 224 million to 872 million and increased its share of the world population from 9% to 14%. On the losing end are Europe, with a halving of its percentage from 16% to 8%, and North America with a decline from 7% in 1950 to only 4% in 2000. Latin America and Asia have slightly increased their share. Due to its quite successful population stabilization policy, the share of the Chinese population in the world has even declined slightly.

Major geographical shifts began to occur in the 17th century with the demise of agrarian societies. The four major agricultural crises in Europe – mostly in Central Europe and the Baltic – between 1844 and 1913 sent out most of the 52 million emigrants who went overseas to settle in thinly populated areas.[1] With the spread of the market economy in the second half of this century, the rural exodus has become pervasive, though with different outcomes, in Latin America, Africa and South Asia.[2]

Projections tend to indicate that migrations will continue to increase in all developing regions, fostered by a combination of factors including the spiral of population growth and poverty; land or wealth concentration; economic polarization in agricultural production; and inefficient, corrupt or mistaken government policies. All of these lead to rural out-migration, loss of livelihoods, land degradation and desertification, and food and land scarcity.

Another important factor, which will very likely increase the importance of the 'pull' factors in rural out-migration, is the spread of a cultural urban bias through education and the mass media. Additionally, if competition for control and access of scarce resources (land, capital, technology, water) increases (especially in rural areas of less developed countries and in Eastern European countries, most probably running along traditional lines of ethnicity and nationalism), political refugees will also most likely increase in numbers. Migration has been a survival strategy for the poor. It seems obvious that people will continue to flow to those areas where wealth, meaning possibilities of livelihoods, amenities and the perception of the 'good life' are concentrated. In the future, major outflows may be expected with increasing climatic events and with cumulative environmental changes that may destroy local people's livelihoods. The first migration would be outflows in Africa,

---

1. Other kinds of outflows have involved fewer numbers: the slave trade across the Atlantic – 6-12 million; political refugees in all countries of the world – 14 million.
2. Perhaps nine-tenths of the population increase in Northern America and Oceania and two-thirds of that in Latin America could be directly attributed to European migrant populations within Europe's demographic outshoots in the vast, formerly thinly populated land of the Americas, Oceania, and North Asia. Altogether, the areas of European settlements that comprised 20% of the world's population in 1700 claimed 36% of that total by the middle of the 20th century.

due to famines and desertification; and it would occur from regions most vulnerable to possible climatic changes, especially coastlines, deltas and islands. At present, more than a million people a year migrate permanently, and almost a million more seek asylum. The number of refugees rose from 2.8 million in 1976 to 17.3 million in 1990 (UNFPA 1993; FAO 1993). According to FAO, as many as 70 million people, mostly from developing countries, are working legally or illegally in other countries. Both internal and international migration are driven by population growth and inequity, and are a symptom of underdevelopment (UNFPA 1993). While urbanization at different levels is a universal trend, the rapid growth of mega-cities is, as we saw, most visible in developing countries.

Carrying Capacity

Various estimates of the global carrying capacity of the earth for people have appeared in the literature, ranging from 7.5 billion (Gilliand, cited in Demeny 1988, 224-5) to 12 billion (Clark 1958), 40 billion (Revelle 1976) and 50 billion (Brown 1954). However, many authors are sceptical about the criteria – amount of food, or kilocalories – used as a basis for these estimates because human levels of resource use and carrying capacity are culturally determined. For example, the global carrying capacity for North Americans would be much lower than the carrying capacity for Indians because each American consumes much more than each Indian does, although this could change rapidly through cultural adaptation.

Carrying capacity is therefore best defined as the total impact of the human population, which is the product of population size and per capita resource use. It is up to us to decide how to divide it between numbers of people and per capita resource use and, in so doing, to establish some minimum standards for quality of life. This complicates population policy enormously, since one cannot simply state a maximum population, but rather must state a maximum number of impact units, which is an indicator of 'sustainable scale', or a one-dimensional equivalent of the 'environmental utilization space' to be discussed in Chapter 3. How many impact units the earth can sustain and how to distribute these impact units over the population is therefore also a social and political question.

Many case studies indicate that 'there is no linear relation between growing population and density, and pressures towards land degradation and desertification' (Caldwell 1982). In fact, one study found that land degradation can occur under rising pressure of population on resources (PPR), under declining PPR and without PPR (Blakie and Brookfield 1987). Clark and his colleagues examined data for 12 countries from 1925 to 1985 and concluded that the same loading of pollution on the environment can come from radically different combinations of population size, consumption and production. Thus no single factor dominates the changing patterns of total impact across time (Arizpe *et al.* 1991). Understanding the patterns of natural resource utilization by the poor also requires an examination of the relative roles of institutions and public policies that shape the structure of incentives to which the poor respond (Jaganathan 1989), an issue taken up in the remainder of this report.

It has repeatedly been shown that the level of fertility in a population cannot be simply regulated but depends crucially on such social and economic changes as improved educational status, especially of women, improvements in social infrastructure and the reduction of poverty. These factors can lead to a lower desired number of children by providing non-maternal roles and greater options for women, and by increasing the costs and lowering the benefits of having large numbers of children. For example, educational opportunities that require school attendance reduce the availability of children for agricultural labour and increase the expenses of raising children (Bongaarts 1994). Policies that focus solely on the control of population size are known to be insufficient, although encouragement of voluntary choice of family size and family planning methods should be applied in both more and less developed countries. The Cairo Conference on Population stressed that the issue of population requires concerted efforts to address and improve living conditions and the socio-economic prospects of the poorest deciles in the range of income distribution with a special focus on improving womens' livelihoods.

For some authors, 'population can only be expected to fall when livelihoods [of the poor] are secure, for only then does it become rational for poor people to limit family size'. According to a World Bank study of 64 countries, when the income of the poor rises by 1%, general fertility rates drop by 3%. When making such statements, however, one must be aware of the great social and cultural heterogeneity among the poor in different parts of the world, which is highly relevant to the way in which their fertility reacts to improving living conditions (Arizpe *et al.* 1991).

Other authors state that 'population is not a relevant variable' in terms of resource depletion, and stress that resource consumption, particularly overconsumption by the affluent, is the key factor. The elasticity of consumption is such that it will increase even with a decrease in population growth. OECD countries represent only 16% of the world's population and 24% of land areas, but their economies account for about 72% of the world gross product, 78% of road vehicles, and 50% of global energy use. They generate about 76% of world trade, 73% of chemical product exports, and 73% of forest product imports (OECD 1993). In the 1980s, developed countries had 22% of the population and generated 91% of the world's industrial waste, 93% of its industrial effluents, 95% of its hazardous waste, 87% of its CFC emissions and 74% of its CO_2 emissions from fossil fuels (Harrison 1992). The main policy instrument, in this case in the short term, is reducing consumption – which can be most easily achieved in those areas where consumption per capita is highest (Arizpe *et al.* 1991).

However, consumption and population growth rates are slowing in the North while increasing rapidly in the South. Fertilizer consumption in the South, as a percentage of the world total, rose from 27.5% to 42% from 1977 to 1988, is expected to be more than 50% by the mid-1990s and 60% by the end of the century. CO_2 emissions from fossil fuels are projected to rise from 26% in 1985 to 44% in 2025 – CO_2 emissions from deforestation are already 100% because northern countries are currently having a net increase in forest area. Also, the distinction between developed and developing countries is increasingly obsolete as the elites of developing countries consume and pollute at the same levels as middle-class westerners. In the United States, the richest 10% of the population contributes 11 times more CO_2 emissions than the poorest 20%, and the poorest 20% in Japan and the United Kingdom contribute about the same as the national average for the people of Chad and Iran, and less than the average Zimbabwean. The wealthiest 10% of Malaysians contribute about the same as the average European; the wealthiest 10% of Columbians the same as the typical Swiss; and the wealthiest 10% of Brazilians more than the average Frenchman (Harrison 1992).

Thus a new framework should expand the definitions of issues – focusing not only on population size, density, rate of increase, age distribution and sex ratios, but also on access to resources, livelihoods, social dimensions of gender and structures of power. New models have to be explored in which population control is not simply a question of family planning but of economic, ecological, social and political planning, in which the wasteful use of resources is not simply a question of finding new substitutes but of reshaping affluent life-styles, and in which sustainability is seen not only as a global aggregate process, but also as one having to do with sustainable livelihoods for the majority of local peoples (Arizpe *et al.* 1991).

The latter view of sustainability brings us back to the more concrete level of issues related to resources and land and urban environments.

Land Degradation

Land degradation may result from wind and water erosion, chemical deterioration or physical deterioration. The direct causes of human-induced land degradation, only partially linked to poverty, include excessive logging, expansion of cropland, overpasturing, reduced fallow periods, uncontrolled wood cutting, monocultural practices, compaction/erosion from mechanized ploughing, excessive and careless use of agrochemicals and irrigation.

The following aspects of land degradation will be discussed below: desertification, deforestation, mining, biodiversity loss, water supply and urbanization.

Desertification

In arid, semi-arid and dry sub-humid lands, human-induced land degradation processes lead to desertification – a primary concern in developing countries because they are mainly located in these types of land areas. Climatic change may alter the frequency and severity of drought and may cause desiccation, but whether desertification occurs depends on the nature of resource management in dryland areas. Desertification itself may contribute to climate change.

Worldwide, drylands total 5,172 million hectares – over 40% of the total global land area, of which 69.5% has been classified as degraded or desertified (Tolba *et al.* 1992; UNEP 1991). The symptoms include: reduction or failure of crop yields, reduction of biomass in rangelands needed as feed material for livestock, reduction of wood biomass (which increases the distance that must be travelled to obtain firewood), reduced water availability, encroachment of sand on productive land and human settlements and societal disruption resulting from environmental deterioration (Tolba *et al.* 1992). Principal land uses in the drylands are irrigated crops, rain-fed croplands, and rangelands. Table 6 shows the amount of degradation attributable to each land use by continent. The key problems in rain-fed croplands have been water and wind erosion, depletion of nutrients and physical deterioration; in irrigated drylands, waterlogging, salinization and alkalinization of soils, aquifer depletion, water quality degradation and increased water-borne diseases; and in rangelands, degradation of vegetation and soil erosion (UNEP 1991; Tolba *et al.* 1992).

Desertification is in part driven by growing population pressure in arid regions, which has in turn led to increased demand for fuelwood and the growing of food crops in areas not suited for agriculture: 900 million hectares (or 20%) of drylands in developing countries have been degraded in this way. It is estimated that 230 million people occupy desertified land and that 850 million live in areas of declining productivity. In sub-Saharan Africa, 65 million hectares have become desertified and are inhabited by 100 million people. These conditions are primarily found in the Sahelian countries, the Horn of Africa, East Africa, most of Southeast Asia, Afghanistan, parts of South Asia, Java, the Philippines, the Andes, northeast Brazil, El Salvador, Guatemala and Haiti. Degradation of upland watersheds through soil erosion also affects prime agricultural areas in the lowlands. Degraded upland areas include the highlands of Ethiopia, the uplands of the Andean region, the upper Himalayan watersheds, the central highlands of Central America, Haiti, the Dominican Republic and other Caribbean countries and are occupied by 500 million people (Leonard 1989).

TABLE 6a

Extent of Desertification in the World's Drylands

		Million hectares	% of total drylands
1	Degraded irrigated lands	43	0.8
2	Degraded rain-fed croplands	216	4.1
3	Degraded rangelands (soil and vegetation degradation)	757	14.6
4	Drylands with human-induced soil degradation (1+2+3 above)	1016	19.5
5	Degraded rangelands (vegetation degradation without soil degradation)	2576	50
6	Total degraded drylands (4+5 above)	3592	69.5
7	Non-degraded drylands	1580	30.5
8	Total area of drylands excluding hyper-arid deserts (978 million ha) (6+7 above)	5172	100

Source: UNEP 1992; Tolba *et al.* 1992.

TABLE 6b

Extent of Desertification in the World's Drylands by Continent

		% desertified in each country					
		Africa	Asia	Australia	Europe	N.America	S.America
1	Degraded irrigated lands	18	35	13	16	28	17
2	Degraded rain-fed croplands	61	56	34	54	16	31
3	Degraded rangelands	74	75	55	72	75	76

Source: UNEP 1992; Tolba *et al.* 1992.

FAO estimates that 5-7 million hectares a year of agricultural land, and 9 million tonnes of grain, are lost to soil erosion, and an additional 1-5 million hectares a year and 1 million tonnes of grain are lost to waterlogging and salinization and alkalinization of irrigated land. One case study in Mali estimated the cost of replacing soil nutrients with imported fertilizer at 40% of net farmer income (FAO 1993).

Although the arid regions and hillsides of developing countries show a strong link between environmental deterioration and food production, it is not always clear to what extent these conditions are caused by direct local impacts of land use practices, and the extent to which they are caused or compounded by the less direct and more global impacts of climate change. The consequences of regional declines in food production, such as famine, may also be caused by problems in social organization, such as lack of adequate transportation, unfair credit systems and failure of the market, as well as war and unrest. For example, in sub-Saharan African countries where there is a significant amount of desertification, agricultural production and GNP both stagnated or declined in the 1980s (Tolba *et al.* 1992). In West Africa, per capita food production declined 25% between 1975 and 1985. However, according to one analysis, this could be attributed to rainfall timing rather than to land degradation. The actual causes of the famine were more likely to be found in the inter-relationships between socio-economic and environmental factors rather than in any particular single factor.

In 1984, a severe famine was reported in the Sudan as a consequence of low agricultural production, although food crops were exported that year. In western Sudan, grain production was only 18-24% of the local need. Although prices increased as a result of low production, farmers did not benefit from this because, in what is known as the 'sheil' agricultural credit system, they had borrowed money from the sheil merchant in exchange for a certain amount of grain from the next harvest. When crops fail, it is the sheil merchant who profits from price increases, while the farmers are left further in debt and without a means of economic recovery. Prices are driven even higher in drought-stricken areas by speculation triggered by rainfall deficits, and it is prohibitively expensive to transport grain to these areas because of poor transportation infrastructure. Relief projects have concentrated on technical rather than socio-economic aspects of agricultural production, and agricultural policies have typically focused on large-scale agriculture for export, ignoring the traditional smallholder agriculture sector, which employed 70-80% of the population and produced a significant amount of food and cash crops.

Deforestation

Forests currently occupy approximately one-third of the earth's land surface (4 million hectares), approximately 15% less than in pre-industrial times. Just over half of world forests (50.7%) are located in developed countries in the temperate zone, the other half are in the undeveloped countries, mostly in the tropics (42.6%) and the remainder (6.7%) are in developing countries in the temperate zone. In the developed countries, forest clearing has slowed down and the overall forested area has increased in this century, although it has continued to decline regionally, in the United States, Canada and Japan. Deforestation has accelerated instead in the developing countries, where it is estimated that forest areas have been halved in this century (Williams 1990).

Tropical forests were estimated to cover just over 1.7 billion hectares in 1990. Preliminary FAO data suggest that tropical deforestation rates averaged close to 1% a year (16.9 million hectares) in the 1980s, and that this represented an increase of approximately 50% from rates calculated for the period of 1976-80. The highest rates were found in Asia (1.2%). Rates for Latin America were 0.9%, and for Africa, 0.8%. South Asia accounts for 20% of world tropical moist forest, of which half is in Indonesia, which also accounts for 85% of the deforestation in Southeast Asia (Barbier and Burgess 1993).

Most tropical deforestation is done for agricultural purposes (FAO 1993). Although some traditional agricultural practices in tropical forests are relatively sustainable under low population densities, shifting agriculture practised by settlers is thought to have accounted for 45% of tropical forest loss in the late 1970s. In 1980, shifting agriculture accounted for 35% of deforestation in Latin America, 70% in Africa and 49% in Southeast Asia (Tolba et al. 1992). Soils in tropical forest areas that have been cleared for agriculture by settlers normally lose most of their fertility within a few years. The settlers are often people who have been relocated to the forest by the government to relieve population pressure elsewhere, or for political reasons. The government also makes these lands accessible by building roads, initially to provide access for logging activities. Much of the land cleared by settlers is actually forest area that has been previously logged. This type of land clearing ultimately benefits large landholders and companies that buy and consolidate small tracts of cleared land, usually for subsidized cattle ranching as the original settlers move on and clear more land. This pattern is not unique to tropical forests in developing countries – rather, it is typical of frontier processes such as those which took place in the Great Plains of the United States in the 1800s.

Deforestation is also driven by the demand for timber and fuelwood. Fuelwood and charcoal production account for about half of all wood consumption (1.4 billion tonnes). Between 30% and 40% of the world's population depends on fuelwood for cooking and warmth because cash is not available for purchasing fossil fuels (Tolba et al. 1992). In 1980, fuelwood accounted for 58% of energy consumption in Africa, 17% in Asia and 8% in Latin America. Among some individual countries, it was 68% in Kenya, 96% in Ethiopia and 98% in Mozambique. Wood provides 17% of all energy consumption in developing countries, and over 70% in the 40 poorest countries. Combined, wood and other forms of biomass fuels provide 35% of all primary energy in developing countries, are relied upon by almost half of the world's population for daily energy needs and contribute 1-3% of greenhouse gasses and other pollutants to the atmosphere. Fossil fuels have not provided a substitute because of price, as well as lack of distribution and access to stoves. According to Barnard (1987):

'Though woodfuel is in principle a renewable resource, the fact is that in many parts of the world it is being depleted just as surely as if it were an irreplaceable fossil fuel. If present trends continue, the woodfuel supplies of many hundreds of millions of people will be exhausted long before the oil fields on which the industrialized world depends have run dry.'

It has been estimated that 1.3 billion people were short of fuelwood in 1980, and it is projected that 2.7 billion will be short by the year 2000 (Tolba et al. 1992). In a 1984 report, FAO found that 69 of 95 developing countries had fuelwood shortages and that those countries with fuelwood shortages that were at risk of desertification also did not have enough land to feed their population (Leonard 1989). The people most acutely affected are in the dry zones of the Sahelian countries, East and Southeast Africa, arid mountainous zones of the Himalayan and Andean countries and arid areas of the Pacific coast and Latin America (Leonard 1989).

Less wood is cut for timber in developing countries than for fuelwood, and most of it is used for domestic consumption, although timber cutting for export is significant in some areas. It is difficult to distinguish between timber production as a by-product of conversion to agriculture and timber-related deforestation *per se*. In Indonesia, close to 50% of production forests are conversion forests. It is estimated that approximately 17% of tropical timber production is used for industrial purposes, of which 31%, or 6% of the total, is exported as roundwood, accounting for 15% of global timber production and 11% of the value of global exports. Forest product exports account for over 10% of the total value of exports from the Central African Republic, Ghana, Indonesia, Malaysia, and Papua New Guinea (Barbier and Burgess, 1993). Three-quarters of tropical timber exports are derived from Malaysia and Indonesia, and 80% is sent to Japan. Because of declining inventory, the market share of tropical hardwood logs is expected to decline with respect to temperate hardwoods – many tropical timber producing countries are already net timber importers (Barbier and Burgess, 1993).

Deforestation leads to the impoverishment of people as well as of the environment because, in addition to providing timber and fuelwood, forests are relied on by many local communities for food, medicine and many non-timber products that provide a means to generate income. Internationally traded non-timber forest products include gums, resins, bamboos, oils, rosin and turpentine, tanning materials, honey, seeds and spices, wildlife products, bark and tree leaves and medicinal plants. Locally and regionally traded products include insects, fruits, fungi, bushmeat, cola nuts and palm wines. They are also the source of locally used materials for building and handicrafts. Palm oils, derived from secondary forests, have even been considered as substitutes for fossil fuels (Duke 1992). Deforestation is also a major threat to indigenous populations who live in forests, who have sustainably managed forest resources, who have the biggest stake in their conservation, and whose knowledge may hold the key to sustainable development.

Mining

Mining is a prerequisite for industrial activities; it supplies the raw materials and has impacts far beyond the mining site because it is associated with the development of infrastructure, processing facilities, contamination of adjacent sites, air pollution, energy requirements and the attraction of migrants. Infrastructure requirements may include roads, railways, and airstrips, as well as power lines, hydroelectric plants and dams. One example is the Carajás iron ore project in eastern Amazonia, financed largely by the World Bank. It involved the construction of a deep-water seaport at São Luis, and a 780-kilometre railroad between the port and the mine, in addition to the development of the iron ore mine itself. If all 34 of the charcoal-burning industrial projects it was proposed to build along the railway corridor were built, they would require 3 million tonnes of charcoal or 14 million tonnes of wood a year for fuel, which would result in the deforestation of 1,500 square km a year. Six of those projects have already been established, including four pig-iron smelters. Withdrawal of government subsidies and the fall of pig-iron prices has, for the moment, removed incentives to build the remaining projects.

The presence of the infrastructure, however, created an incentive for uncontrolled development in the region, in the form of cattle ranching, logging, shifting cultivation, and gold mining, which resulted in invasions of the indigenous land areas that were to be legally protected. The town of Marab, where two of the smelters were built, and adjacent to the Tucurui electric dam, grew from 60,000 to 260,000 inhabitants in the 1980s. In this town, 70% of the adults are illiterate, 25,000 children have no access to schools, more than 60% of homes are without running water, less than a third have electricity, and city water sources are contaminated with mercury used in gold mining. In addition, in 1989, there were 6,000 cases of malaria, 7,500 cases of tuberculosis or leprosy, and high levels of hepatitis, typhoid fever and intestinal infections. Forests to the east were being cut to fuel the cast-iron mills and pig-iron smelters located in the city, and to the south is an area with the highest number of deaths resulting from land conflicts in the Amazon region. An evaluation conducted by the World Bank Operations Evaluation Department concluded that the project catalysed large-scale deforestation and 'played an important role in contributing to increased land concentration and poverty, extensive public health problems, increased rural violence, and... to increased malnutrition and reduced food security for large numbers of poor'.

Effects of the mining process itself may include alteration of the local hydrology and water tables, contamination of surface and groundwater with acid mine drainage, sediment run-off, sewage and mineral effluents, destruction of habitat, changes in the landform and land instability. Mine tailings, which are the residue after metals are extracted from the ore, contain the remains of the minerals and of the potentially toxic chemicals and inorganic reagents (e.g., zinc and copper sulphates, sodium cyanide and sodium dichromate) used in the extraction process including, in some cases, significant amounts of sulphides which become transformed into sulphuric acid and poison aquatic life. Tailings may consist of up to 90% of the ore and are one of the largest sources of solid wastes, although the actual amount depends on the grade or metal content of an ore. They are left in piles or in ponds, where they release formerly bound contaminants through the leaching process (e.g., arsenic, cadmium, copper, lead and zinc). Other effects include air pollution from particles, gases and vapours, ecosystem damage, degradation resulting from inadequate rehabilitation at closure, failure of structures and dams, abandoned equipment and buildings, dust emissions from sites near living areas, release of methane from mines, occupational impacts from dust inhalation, fugitive emissions within the plant, air emissions in confined spaces, exposure to toxic materials used on site, heat and noise vibration, physical risks, unsanitary living conditions, as well as aesthetic and socio-economic effects (UNEP 1993; Tolba *et al.* 1992).

Although developed countries account for most metal consumption, significant amounts of mining and processing occur in the developing countries and these activities are expanding, in part to meet the consumption needs of the developed countries and in part because of industrial expansion in the developing countries themselves. It was the depletion of mineral reserves and the search for new deposits that helped give rise to imperialism and to 'large corporations able to raise capital in London and New York to spend half a world away' (Headrick 1990). As is discussed further in the section on unequal exchange, one of the characteristics of mining is that it provides few if any benefits to local populations. According to

Headrick, 'the oil industry was so capital-intensive and used so little unskilled labor that several oil-producing countries like Mexico and Burma saw their resources depleted with almost no national impact.... Not until the 1970s did underdeveloped but oil-rich countries in the middle East, Africa, and Latin America receive benefits from their resources comparable to those that the industrialized customers had long been enjoying.' Mining has been called an 'enclave' economy because it normally takes place in remote areas in which whole towns, railroads and harbours are created that are more closely related to distant markets than to their surroundings, and which only last as long as the mineral resources (Headrick 1990). As these are depleted, both the land and the people are left impoverished.

Loss of Biodiversity

It has been estimated, based on habitat loss, that 27,000 species a year are currently being lost in tropical forests alone. Together with other habitats, primarily coral reefs, wetlands, islands and montane environments, the total is estimated at 30,000 a year. The biggest threat to biodiversity is the loss and modification of habitat because of clearing for agriculture and human settlement, and for logging. Coral reefs, also found in the tropics, are threatened by nutrient enrichment from sewage inputs and soil leaching, mining, fishing, siltation and sedimentation from the washing out of unprotected soils from deforested land to coastal waters.

An analysis conducted by the World Conservation Monitoring Centre found that most protected areas are in regions that are not intensively developed to begin with, such as mixed mountain and island systems. The much lower representation of temperate grasslands and lake systems that are intensively used by humans suggests that socio-economic and political factors have played an important role in the selection of protected areas, and that there is a need to develop socio-economic incentives for conservation and to encourage local communities to be involved in the development of conservation strategies.

There is a profound link between biodiversity and poverty because the highest levels of both poverty and biodiversity are found in developing countries. The highest levels of agricultural biodiversity are found between 20° and 45° North, in proximity to major mountain ranges. Mountains have a high degree of ecological heterogeneity and variability because they contain numerous micro-environmental zones which lead to high speciation, making them centres of diversity for both cultivated plants and human cultures. The genetic origins of the 30 crop plants that provide 95% of all human nutritional requirements are found in Asia, Africa, and Latin America. Biodiversity is also important as the source of medicinal plants used in traditional as well as in modern medicine systems. According to FAO, Brazil has at least 3,000 recorded medicinal plants, India has more than 2,000 and Malaysia has approximately 1,000. For at least three-quarters of the world population, and possibly as much as 90%, traditional medicine is the only medical treatment available (FAO 1993).

Wild parents of modern domesticated crops are difficult to gather and collect because they 'shatter' – a process by which seeds are highly dispersed. Their domestication for agriculture was made possible by the first farmers who collected anomalous plants in which the seeds cling to the plant, and subsequently harvested and sowed non-shattering seeds. Non-shattering seeds, in turn, rely on cultivation for their propagation. Continuation of this process also led to high genetic biodiversity in food crops, and to cultural diversity – because a community which is dependent on particular resources for its survival generates a very deep understanding of the patterns of variation in those resources. For example, approximately 3,000 varieties of potato are grown in the Andes region, of which up to 45 varieties may be found in a single field. This variety is recognized in the individual names they have been given by the Quechua people who cultivate them.

Agricultural biodiversity provides a form of insurance against pests and diseases and is the basis for adaptation to environmental change in our agricultural systems. It is threatened by the spread of modern varieties of corn, wheat, rice and other crops, and the monocrop agricultural systems introduced by the Green Revolution – in Indonesia alone, 1,500 local rice varieties have become extinct in the last 15 years (WRI 1992). According to FAO, it is essential to conserve the broadest possible range of genetic diversity because 'Future gains in agricultural production will depend on how plant and animal breeders use genetic diversity to introduce crop varieties and livestock that are less susceptible to environmental stress, able to convert energy and feed more efficiently, are more resistant to diseases and pests, able to supply the diverse range of products needed, and are better able to cope with changes in production and consumer requirements' (FAO 1993).

There is a heavy genetic dependence of the North on the South, and on the uncompensated contributions of the poor, because it is this diversity, and the understanding of it, which provides resistance to diseases, pests and extreme weather, to which modern commercial agriculture is particularly vulnerable. Russians found hardy winter wheats in the Himalayas, and genetic resistance to the southern corn leaf blight, which cost $1 billion in lost corn yield in the United States alone, was found in Mayorbala maize from Africa, although maize originated in Central America. Wild tomato species have provided a source of genes resistant to leaf mold, particular viruses, nematodes, and other diseases. Tropical plants, often used as medicines and poisons by indigenous people, have also led to the development of biodegradable pesticides such as rotenone. This knowledge may be quite sophisticated and require an understanding not just of individual components but of interactions among species and their combined use. For example, 'the preparation of an arrow poison in the northeast Amazon may involve the mixing of seven different species, and the Indians insist that each plant changes and amplifies the toxicity of the poison' (Plotkin 1988). Because of increasing vulnerability in agricultural crops, it is estimated that germplasm from Third World countries currently contributes over $2 billion a year to United States wheat, rice and maize production. Categories superimposed by modern institutions and markets undermine the coping mechanisms built upon indigenous understandings of diversity. Because the products of biodiversity are irregular in shape, size, colour, taste and smell, there is no consumer preference in the modern market for these products, and the producers do not have purchasing power. Unless consumers start demanding, consuming and paying for diverse products which are also better for human health, it will be difficult to conserve biodiversity in fringe areas. In a sense, people may be poor because they know too much – that is, they know more than markets can value and price (Gupta 1992).

Water Quality and Supply
Clean fresh water and access to it are key factors that limit the potential for growth because water is essential for human health and welfare as well as for agricultural and industrial production. Water scarcity primarily affects the major arid and semi-arid regions where most poverty is located – Africa, the Middle East and South Asia. Access, however, depends on infrastructure for distribution and on socio-economic factors related to allocation and management, as well as on supply. Currently 1 billion people do not have access to running water, and 1.7 billion are without sanitation facilities, placing them at risk from water-related diseases. As a scarce resource that crosses political boundaries, water is also, increasingly, a source of international conflict. Political boundaries fragment management of the resource and create inequities in access, which are most evident on borders between developed and developing countries such as that between the United States and Mexico. International river basins also fall disproportionately in developing countries.

Water resources are only renewable if the consumption rate is lower than the recharge rate, which depends on the source from which it is obtained. Groundwater, for example, is renewed at the average rate of once every 1,400 years, compared with every 8 days for atmospheric moisture, 16 days for stream water, 1 year for soil moisture, 5 years for swamps, and 17 years for lakes. The amount of groundwater that can be extracted each year is determined on the basis of each year's recharge. The most renewable source of fresh water is run-off, which consists of the amount of water obtained from rainfall after subtracting evaporation.

In areas of high evaporation this amount can be very small (e.g., in Africa run-off is approximately one-fifth of rainfall), although it can be increased by collecting it and using it as close to the source as possible, in practices referred to as 'water harvesting'. Because of uneven distribution, only a portion of run-off is accessible for human use. It has been estimated that the optimum level of use is 5% of run-off and that water supply may become a limiting factor in development when 20% of run-off is the consumed level (Clarke 1993). Withdrawal of groundwater faster than the recharge rate may further reduce the water supply because it may lead to saltwater intrusion into the aquifer (WHO 1992).

The current global consumption of water, 400 km^3 a year, is approximately 44% of reliable run-off and has doubled twice since 1940 (Clarke 1993). This amounts to an average of approximately 73 m^3 a year per person, globally, although in developed countries, per capita consumption ranges from 500 to over 2,000 m^3, while in many developing countries it ranges between 20 and 50 m^3 (WHO 1992).

Household water consumption accounts for 7% of total water withdrawal (WHO 1992) and varies depending on the amount of time required to procure it. For example, a survey in Nigeria showed that per capita use was 21 litres a day in an area where it had to be carried, and 82.1 litres for urban users to whom it was readily available. In Swaziland, consumption ranged from 5 litres a day per person, leaving very little for washing either people or dishes, to 13 litres for families who could pay for delivered water, and 30-100 litres for tap users. At the currently estimated 100 litres per capita per day, household water needs could be met from run-off even in the most arid regions. Because of the intensity of water use in sewage systems, it is estimated that household consumption could rise to 150 m^3 per capita by the end of the century as access to safe drinking water and sanitation increases (Clarke 1993).

Industrial use, including in the energy sector, is approximately four times domestic use and accounts for up to 80% of water use in developed countries, but for only a small percentage of water use in developing countries (WHO 1992). Even a small percentage, however, may be locally significant in arid regions. In India, for example, industry accounts for 1.4 km^3 of water a year, domestic demand is double that amount, for livestock and power stations triple that amount, and irrigation uses 360 times as much water or 97% of all use. In Maharashtra State, boreholes were deepened to provide 50,000 litres of water a day to the sugar factories, but they ran dry within a year. Deeper boreholes were sunk (down to 60 m) but they also went dry within a year. In addition, over 2,000 wells in the area went dry, leaving 23,000 villages without a source of drinking water. Industry is also a large contributor to pollution in both developed and developing countries.

Seventy per cent of India's rivers are polluted by industrial waste, and many major rivers in Malaysia have been officially declared dead. Seventy per cent of water consumption is for irrigated agriculture, which comprises 18% of total cropland but produces one-third of the world food supply (WHO 1992). It is increasingly derived from pumping groundwater. When groundwater is pumped faster than its rate of renewal, water tables fall and the costs of pumping go up. Irrigation is also an inefficient process, as less than half of the water used actually reaches the crops and is polluted by salts and nitrates before returning to rivers and aquifers (Clarke 1993). Losses during distribution also occur in cities: for example, unaccounted-for water was found to range from 39% to 67% in a survey of Latin American cities (WHO 1992).

The key sources of water pollution are sewage, industrial effluents, storm and urban run-off and agricultural run-off. Water quality in the urban areas of developing countries has declined because of inadequate sanitation systems and garbage collection and disposal, and because of the failure to enforce pollution controls at point of delivery sources. On the Ganges River in India, for example, there are 114 cities of over 50,000 inhabitants that release untreated sewage; in addition, untreated liquid waste is released from DDT factories, tanneries, pulp and paper mills, petrochemical and fertilizer complexes and rubber factories. The Tiete River that passes through São Paulo, Brazil, is estimated to receive 300 tonnes of effluent a day, containing high levels of heavy metals, from 1,200 industries, and 900 tonnes of sewage, of which only 12.5% is treated. Run-off from agricultural lands has major impacts on water quality because of land clearing, the use of pesticides and fertilizers, and from irrigation (WHO 1992).

Declining fish catches as a result of water pollution have been reported in Malaysia, Lake Maryut in Alexandria, the Bay of Dakar, the Indus delta near Karachi, and in many Chinese rivers. In addition to aquatic ecosystem disturbances, polluted water is estimated to be responsible for illness in half of the population of developing countries and 80% of all illness in those countries (WHO 1992). Poor water quality can also affect rates of deforestation and air quality because of the need to burn more wood to boil drinking water, (Briscoe 1993). Concentrations of pesticides in drinking water have been found to be much higher than WHO guidelines in a number of developing countries (WHO 1992).

Diseases associated with water in developing countries fall into four categories (WHO 1992):

- waterborne diseases – associated with water contaminated by human and animal waste which, if ingested, may lead to cholera, typhoid, and diarrhoeal diseases;
- water-washed diseases – associated with water scarcity or inaccessibility,

which makes it difficult to maintain personal cleanliness, and leads to diarrhoeal diseases and contagious skin and eye infections, as well as waterborne diseases and infestation with lice or mites that may also be vectors of typhus;

- water-based diseases – associated with parasites that pass part of their life-cycle in water, such as schistosomiasis; and

- water-related diseases – associated with insect vectors of disease for which water provides habitat. These may vary according to the type of habitat. For example, mosquitoes that transmit malaria breed in clean water, while those that transmit filiarasis breed in flooded pit latrines and polluted water. Simulium blackflies that spread riverblindness breed in moving water, and Chrysops deerflies that transmit eyeworm breed in muddy swamps.

Untreated sewage in rivers is the major cause of health problems in developing countries. Safe levels of coliform concentration in drinking water are 100 organisms per 100 ml – humans excrete 2 billion per day per capita. Levels above 3 million per 100 ml have been found in the canals in Jakarta and in Nigerian ponds, 7.3 million have been found in the river downstream from the capital of Colombia, and 24 million in the Yamuna River in India after passing New Delhi, compared with a previous count of 7,500. (Clarke 1993). Most funds invested in sewage are used for collection rather than treatment and less than 10% of sewage is treated (Briscoe 1993). Diarrhoeal diseases associated with untreated sewage kill 4 million children a year and are the leading cause of infant and child mortality. The highest levels of cholera are in Africa (for which 134,953 cases and 12,618 deaths were reported for 1991), and in Asia (6,700 cases and 68 deaths) where it is endemic, although in 1991 there was also an unexpected severe outbreak in Latin America (over 300,000 cases and over 3,000 deaths) (WHO 1992).

Schistosomiasis is often associated with dam construction and irrigation – for example, the incidence rose from 6% to 60% following construction of the first Aswan Dam, and from 0% to 90% after the construction of the Volta Dam (WHO 1992). Although the numbers of deaths it causes are relatively low (200,000), those infected (200 million) suffer a marked reduction in productivity, and 600 million are at risk. Malaria causes over 1 million deaths a year and is associated with irrigation and large bodies of standing water (WHO 1992), with deforestation, mining, overcrowded settlements, inadequate sanitation and poor drainage, as well as drought, famine and desertification (Tolba et al. 1992).

The increasing health and economic costs associated with declining water quality and availability have the greatest impacts on the poor. In addition to disease, these costs include the energy costs for boiling drinking water, time spent procuring it, or the increased cost of purchasing it from water vendors. Obtaining water supplies has been estimated as taking up 15% of a woman's time. Poor people with no water connection may pay more than middle class people who have hookups. These expenses were estimated to account for approximately 20% of household budgets in Port-au-Prince, Haiti. Costs of boiling water during the cholera epidemic in Peru were estimated to be 29% of average household income in the squatter settlements (Briscoe 1993). According to WHO (1992), the thriving informal market for water is evidence of an unsatisfied demand, and of how much people would be willing to pay for an adequate conventional water supply if it were made available to them.

Water is increasingly a source of conflict because upstream users may deprive those downstream. When it flows across political boundaries, those downstream may also be externalized from the decision-making process. Borders fragment management strategies for such transboundary resources as water, and may separate problems from their source and from the sites where solutions could most effectively be implemented. Borders also create perverse economic incentives related to trade advantages, cause inequity of access to shared resources and impede problem-solving at the local and regional levels based on shared community interests, because they require decisions to be made through remote, national level political institutions. In general, borders also bear the brunt of environmental degradation and its social costs because they are remote from the centres of political power. The United States border with Mexico, for example, provides a stark example of the differences between North and South. Many polluting industries from the United States are located right on the United States/Mexican border for the sole purpose of taking advantage of these disparities.

Urbanization

Urbanization has implications for the scale and patterns of resource consumption, because it concentrates and increases the demand for energy and resources demands and requires outside sources for input as well as assimilative capacity for waste output. However, urban areas can also reduce rural population pressure and may provide efficiencies and cost advantages in providing such services as piped water, sanitation, waste management, education and health care – if effective government policies are implemented to provide them. In the absence of effective policies, urbanization aggravates environmental and health problems, particularly for the poor, because it increases the concentration of industrial, residential and commercial wastes (WHO 1992).

Currently, 43% of the world population is urban, which includes 72.7% of the population in developed countries, and 34% of the population in developing countries (UNEP 1992); this last percentage is likely to increase to 51% by 2000 and to 65% by 2025 (UN 1991). Urban population in developing countries is growing much faster than in developed countries. From 1950 to 1990, the urban population in developing countries increased by 1.97 billion compared to 430 million in developed countries, the annual growth rate in the late 1980s being 3.8% compared to 1%. The growth rate of cities in developing countries is also twice the overall rate of population growth – 60% is contributed by the natural growth of urban populations, and the remainder is from rural migration to urban areas. In 1960, seven of the world's ten largest urban agglomerations were in North America, Japan and Europe, with New York, Tokyo and London at the top. Presently Tokyo is the largest with 25 million, but seven of the top ten are in less developed countries.

It is difficult to estimate the overall numbers of people who live in inadequate housing in developing countries, but case studies in some large cities show that it is common for 30% to 60% of the population of a city to live in illegal settlements with little or no infrastructure or services, in overcrowded, deteriorating tenements, or in cheap boarding houses (WHO 1992). According to another estimate, 1 billion people currently live in urban squatter settlements, and it is estimated that 60% of city dwellers will be squatters by the end of the 20th century. Another 100 million have no shelter at all, many of them street children (Campbell 1989). Squatter settlements are often found in areas that are subject to natural and man-made hazards such as floods, mudslides, diseases caused by lack of access to water and sanitation, or industrial disasters. For example, squatter settlements on steep slopes where vegetation is destroyed destabilize the hillside and are then subject to mudslides; lack of sewers and site drainage may lead to the formation of pools of contaminated water; flooding may cause latrines to overflow; and uncollected solid wastes may be disposed of in open spaces where they contribute to health problems, block drainage channels and are a health hazard to children. Absence of building codes leads to unsafe building structures that have a greater risk of fire, collapse and electrocution (WHO 1992).

In urban areas, 170 million people lack access to safe and adequate water supplies, and 331 million lack adequate sanitation. This may understate the problem, however, because a water tap within 100 metres of a house may be considered adequate by official agencies but is not necessarily adequate for good health. When there are relatively few water taps in a community, water consumption may be reduced because of the amount of time required to stand in line in order to obtain it, or the tap may only function intermittently for a few hours a day. The quality is often poor because of distribution through contaminated and leaky pipes. Local specialists have found it difficult to reconcile some official figures with what they have witnessed in the field; for example, claims of 100% coverage of the urban populations in Nigeria and Liberia, and 90% in Togo (WHO 1992). Most urban centres in Africa and Asia, including those with over a million inhabitants, have no sewage system at all. Garbage collection is inadequate or nonexistent.

It has been shown that morbidity and mortality rates are related to the amount of household water flow. Squatter settlements near a city show much higher infant mortality rates and incidences of disease than the city as a whole, because of poor housing conditions and a lack of safe water and sanitation facilities. For example, child mortality among the urban poor in northeastern Brazil who do not have water was found to be 50% higher than among urban poor who had water (Campbell 1989).

In addition to the specific health effects associated with inadequate and contaminated water supplies described in the previous section are those associated with overcrowding, indoor and outdoor air pollution, disease vectors found in urban environments, and household accidents. Overcrowding facilitates the spread of airborne infections, pneumonia, tuberculosis and other respiratory infections, which may also be aggravated by dampness and indoor air pollution. Acute bacterial and viral respiratory infections and tuberculosis account for 5 million deaths a year and are more prevalent in urban than in rural areas. The environment around human dwellings provides habitat to several kinds of insects and rodents that carry a wide variety of diseases such as malaria, typhoid, yellow fever and Chagas. They may breed on the body surface or in clothes (e.g., lice and scabies), in the house (fleas, cockroaches, bedbugs, triatomine bugs and soft ticks), in containers and in sewage (mosquitoes, midges and flies), or may enter the house to feed (mosquitoes, sandflies and scorpions). Chagas is a disease transmitted by bugs that flourish in cracks and crevices of poor-quality housing that is estimated to affect 500,000 people a year in Latin America and from which 18 million people currently suffer. A large number of people in low-income settlements also have intestinal worms. Scavengers, who extract saleable material from waste and recycle it, usually have chronic skin, eye and respiratory diseases and frequent intestinal problems. Seven hundred million women and children have greater exposure to indoor air pollution from using biomass fuels for cooking, which is a cause of respiratory infections and chronic obstructive pulmonary disease. Accidents are another major cause of illness and injury and were found to account for 19% of health problems in a survey of 559 slum children in Rio (WHO 1992; Tolba *et al.* 1992).

The highest levels of air pollution are found in developing countries, in which were sited 17 of the worst 20 cities for smoke particles in the early 1980s – Jakarta, Delhi, Beijing and Shenyang all had ranges above 200 micrograms per m^3, and Lahore had almost 800, compared to 53-89 in New York and 22-44 in Frankfurt. Associated respiratory illnesses mostly afflict the poor, who often cannot afford to live in areas safely distanced from smoke-stacks. They also suffer the most from city congestion, because they often live far from where they work, and must use slow public transport. It was estimated that in Bogotá the average low-income adult spends 127 minutes per day commuting, 44 minutes more than high-income travellers. Much of the congestion is caused by cars, taxis or rickshaws used by the more wealthy citizens, which take up significantly more road space per passenger than buses. In Karachi, cars cover 44% of passenger miles but use up to 83% of road space. In Manila, cars and taxis account for 54% of all vehicle trips but contribute only 30% of person trips.

In spite of all these conditions, people continue to move to Third World cities for better income and job opportunities. Although industrial output has risen in less developed countries, it has not provided the employment opportunities it provided in industrializing countries in the 19th century, although people are finding work in the informal sector, which has low capital requirements and high labour inputs.

In a study that examined the relationship between environmental degradation and urban growth rates in 65 developing countries, woodfuel use, safe drinking water, subsistence food production and population pressure were found to be critical factors in explaining urban migration (Somma 1991). For example, urban growth was significantly higher where the rural population had a lower availability of safe drinking water than the urban areas, where there was a high level of pressure on woodfuel resources, and declining per capita food consumption. The most powerful predictor of ecological flight, however, was a high rate of infant mortality. Africa, which has the highest rates of environmental degradation in terms of unsafe drinking water, high infant mortality, declines in food production per capita and high fuelwood consumption, also has the highest rates of urban growth. Tanzania, Burundi, Kenya, Malawi, Rwanda and Mozambique have urban growth rates that range from 7.4% to 9.2% a year. In contrast, China, Sri Lanka, Jamaica and Panama have both lower urban growth rates (1.7% to 2.9%) and lower rates of environmental degradation (Somma 1991).

Impacts of Environmental Stress and Resource Exploitation on the Poor

Shifting Environmental Costs to the Poor

Direct links between environmental quality and resource endowments in developing countries on the one hand and poverty on the other, were explored above. In addition to the effects on the poor of local degradation of land and water supplies poor people also pay a disproportionate share of the costs of global-scale environmental degradation caused primarily by the rich.

For example, even though crop declines associated with human-induced climate change are expected to be small, negative yields are primarily found in the low latitude countries, where most developing countries are located. Sea-level rise would hit hardest on agricultural societies in coastal plains, the main source of grains in low latitude countries, and in island nations in the Pacific.

The poor are also disproportionately affected by the decline in world fish stocks because the poorest two-thirds of the world's population gets 40% of its protein from fish. The artisanal fisheries of the less developed countries also employ 20 times more people than are employed by the industrial fisheries. This decline is associated primarily with overfishing, marine pollution and, potentially, with the loss of stratospheric ozone, which may damage fish at the larval stage and plankton that form the basis of the marine food chain. It is the developed countries, however, that have encouraged overfishing through subsidies to the fishing industry, which has grown twice as fast as the global catch. The fish catch has increased five times since 1950 by fishing in new seas, increasingly off the coasts of Third World countries, which may not have the equipment to exploit them nor the capacity to enforce quotas on foreign fleets from the North. Although there is a steadily rising demand for fish as a source of protein in the South, the greatest increase in demand is from the North, where almost one-third of the global fish catch is processed into oil, fish meal and fertilizer. Fish meal is used as a feed supplement for livestock, and fertilizer is used to cultivate grains, of which a significant portion is used as livestock feed.

Much of the increased consumption is driven by cities that must import most of their food, fuel, building materials and water from increasing distances, which leads to higher packaging, processing and transportation costs, greater competition for resources with agriculture and forestry, increased use of commercial energy inputs in agriculture and rural impoverishment.

Indigenous populations in the Arctic regions of the far north are exposed to disproportionately high levels of organochlorines, most notably PCBs, radionuclides and other toxic contaminants generated primarily in the industrial countries (Barrie et al. 1992). Although pathways and processes may differ for different classes of chemicals, at least for organochlorines exposure appears to be the result of long-term processes of transfer from warmer to colder regions (Muir et al. 1992), where the toxins have become concentrated in the food chain in the traditional foods of indigenous populations in the far north, and in the breast milk of women in some northern communities. A pilot study in one indigenous community, on Broughton Island, found that 73% of the population had intake levels of PCBs above the Canadian 'tolerable daily intake', and that the highest levels were in children and in women. A major concern is intrauterine exposure and levels of ingestion by breast-fed infants. Although the PCB concentrations are lower in marketed foods, and assuming the population was able to obtain more access to marketed foods, switching from a traditional subsistence diet of harvest foods to imported market foods would not necessarily benefit that population because they do not provide the same nutritional benefits and are associated with risks of obesity, diabetes, cardiovascular disease and cancer (Kinloch *et al.* 1992).

Developed countries produce most of the world's waste, although the quantity of waste has a close correlation to income, regardless of whether it is produced in developed or less developed countries. There are also cultural differences. For example, the average European and Japanese produce less waste than the average North American at the same income level. Yet more than 90% of hazardous wastes are generated in OECD countries. Because of increased environmental concerns and the high cost of disposal in developed countries, much of this waste is being exported to developing countries who do not have proper facilities for treating it, nor clear waste management policies (UNDP 1993). Some toxic waste export deals reported to have taken place in over 20 African countries, legally and illegally, included an offer of $50 per tonne to the government of Guinea, $40 per tonne to Guinea-Bissau, and $2.50 per tonne to Benin, as one time payments – compared to up to $4,000 per tonne for legal disposal in the United States. Although shipments of hazardous wastes from developed to developing countries have been widely reported in the press, it is difficult to document the extent of the practice. Based on written and oral reports, OECD suggests a ballpark figure of several hundred thousand tonnes (UNDP 1993). Monitoring of publicly available information regarding exports by ship conducted by the non-governmental organization Greenpeace, suggests that most hazardous waste exports are destined for South Asia and Central and Eastern Europe, because of bans elsewhere. Between January and August 1993, over 36,000 tonnes of hazardous wastes were sent to Asia through the ports of the northwestern United States, including at least 1,800 tonnes of banned or never-registered pesticides. These figures also only reflect wastes that have been properly classified. Often, exported hazardous waste is classified as primary production material for recycling and recovery operations (which leave a residue of equally or more hazardous wastes and expose workers and the environment to these substances) in countries with weak or nonexistent standards for human and environmental protection. According to United States Customs shipping records, almost half of United States pesticide exports in 1991, more than 26,000 tonnes, were either banned, suspended, never registered or had restricted use in the United States.

In addition to transporting wastes, many of the most polluting and energy-intensive industries are growing faster in less developed countries or are relocating there. These include the iron and steel, non-ferrous metals, non-metallic minerals, chemical, pulp and paper industries. From 1980 to 1985, they grew twice as fast in developing countries as in developed countries. The chlorine industry, which is associated with all organochlorine-based products, such as pesticides, plastics, solvents and refrigerants, is in the process of a major shift to developing countries. Seventy per cent of the annual production of 45 million tonnes currently takes place in North America and Europe, but new facilities are being located in Asia and Latin America. One view on this is that in this way developing countries are making use of the comparative advantages that they have over developed countries in terms of differences in environmental standards or qualities. In this way, they can benefit economically from the environmental problems in developed countries by taking over parts of economic activities that traditionally were located in the North. However, this process may amount to redistributing environmentally risky activities to countries where often the population at large has little knowledge and awareness of the risks involved. A resolution passed by the American Public Health Association in October 1993, which supports a broad phase-out of this class of chemicals, notes that 'virtually all chlorinated organic compounds that have been studied exhibit at least one of a wide range of serious toxic effects such as endocrine dysfunction, developmental impairment, birth defects, reproductive dysfunction and infertility, immunosuppression and cancer, often at extremely low doses'. Exposure to pesticides, toxic fumes, hazardous wastes and hazardous processes causes poor working conditions and may result in serious accidents as well as chronic health effects on workers and on the community – adding to the already staggering health effects from lack of water and sanitation facilities. These effects are difficult to estimate because symptoms might not be associated with the correct causes. However, WHO estimates that, in developing countries, 3 million people suffer from the effects of single short-term exposure, including 220,000 deaths, and over 700,000 people a year may be suffering from the chronic effects of long-term exposure (WHO 1992).

As discussed in this section, it is the poor who pay most of the externalized non-market social costs of environmental degradation resulting from what we might also call the process of pollution 'trickle down'. This is because poor people live in marginal areas and are marginal to the decision-making process. As stated by Tolba *et al.* (1992): 'Hazardous wastes tend to "run downhill" to the least regulated and least expensive disposal option unless market forces are such that they direct hazardous waste management to more appropriate options.' In general, consumption by developed countries of the earth's capacity to absorb pollution has preempted development options for poor countries. Unlike 19th-century Europeans, citizens of developing countries are unable to migrate legally to less populated continents. Even in the 19th century, however, this process displaced many people and was accompanied by a significant amount of violence – a process that could be repeated if the global economy continues in the direction of greater inequity.

Environmental Degradation and Community Deterioration

Perhaps the most insidious effect of human-induced environme..
deterioration of communities, evidenced by the loss of reciproci.,
community members. Unlike the rekindling of community ties through mutua.
assistance normally experienced after natural disasters, communities traumatized
by human-induced environmental disasters are characterized instead by
divisiveness between those affected and those not affected, and the loss of trust,
respect, decency, charity and concern that normally bind human communities in
times of crisis. They may be drawn together instead by a shared pessimism
(Erikson 1994).

Part of what appears to set these disasters apart is the denial of responsibility by
those in charge and the absence of any apology. The corporations within which
environmental hazards have occurred are legal entities established for the purpose
of shielding stockholders from financial liability and therefore personal and moral
responsibility. Thus, it is cynical that Union Carbide has had its highest profits on
record in the aftermath of the 1984 Bhopal disaster (Hager 1991). 'The real
problem in the long run is that the inhumanity people experience comes to be seen
as a natural feature of human life rather than as the bad manners of a particular
corporation. They think their eyes are being opened to a larger and profoundly
unsettling truth: that human institutions cannot be relied on' (Erikson 1994).

Thus, environmental disasters may result in the corrosion of communities and
the loss of reciprocity. This reciprocity is one of the sources of security in
communities that do not have public social security systems to fall back upon.
Moreover, environmental disasters may increase divisiveness among communities.
Thirdly, there exists a lack of responsiveness on the part of national governments
and international agencies to the lot of such unempowered communities. And
finally: one of the consequences of the above-mentioned factors is that such
communities begin to self-destruct, showing signs of destroying their human and
natural capital. In this way a new dimension is also added to the trauma of poverty.

The Institutionalization of Poverty and Environmental Degradation

Poverty as a Social Trap

Poverty may be considered as the most profound social trap. A social trap is any
situation in which the short-run, local reinforcements guiding individual behaviour
are inconsistent with the long-run, global best interests of the individual and
society. Social traps are situations in which the short-term, local optimizing of
individuals goes afoul. In this sense, they indicate imperfections in the unregulated
free market approach to resource allocation, which relies on short-term, local

optimizing of individuals. It may be argued that the role of a democratic government is to eliminate social traps (no more and no less), while maintaining as much individual freedom as possible, in situations where social forces will not on their own lead to a social optimum or only at relatively high transaction costs.

Social traps abound in environmental issues because of the absence of well-defined property rights and the pervasiveness of environmental externalities. Social traps are analogous to what has become known as the 'tragedy of the commons', in which there is a breakdown or absence of institutional mechanisms for cooperation and the resolution of conflicts between individual and community interests in the management of common property resources. Institutions determine and limit access to resources that might otherwise be considered open to access, in order to reduce uncertainties regarding the behaviour of others and to avoid the 'tragedy of the commons'. The time-frame applied to the management of natural resources may be seen as a function of assurances of access and future returns, as well as assurances regarding the behaviour of others and the nature of the resources. For example, it may be rational for a local community recklessly to cut its forest if the timber is also being cut by government forestry agencies or outside contractors over which the community has no control.

A Socio-ecological Model of Household Behaviour

The degree of variability in social interactions depends, to some extent, upon the degree of environmental variability, and is reflected in household preferences and risk-adjustment strategies. In high-risk environments with a high degree of ecological variability, a 'household portfolio approach' can be used to illustrate the diversification in resource use that is an essential component of household survival strategies, particularly where fluctuations in the environment require flexibility in the patterns of household resource allocation. Variability in resource use and survival strategies can be examined with a conceptual model that links household preferences with the ecological context (Gupta 1985 a,b,c). The mix of enterprises of different classes of households evolving in the given context of ecological conditions and access to factor and product markets can be classified on the basis of the average returns from a technology and the variance in these returns over time and space. Thus we may have four kinds of portfolios: High Average Returns-High Variance (Type 1), High Average Returns-Low Variance (Type 2), Low Average Returns-High Variance (Type 3) and Low Average Returns-Low Variance (Type 4). Returns may be stable or unstable, and the household budget may be in surplus, deficit or subsistence, depending on the type of portfolio. Households that have Type 3 portfolios will be the most vulnerable and disadvantaged. Given an initial portfolio and its mean-variance or risk-return characteristics, households may

respond to given risk in the environment through the following alternative means:
(a) household level risk adjustments;
(b) public and market risk-reducing mechanisms, and
(c) communal and common property risk adjustments.

The household risk adjustments include measures that a household can take by negotiation, such as asset disposal, migration and a reduction or modification of family consumption; they may also include strategies such as tenancy, borrowing, labour contracts, and group ploughing.

Public risk-adjustment mechanisms imply the availability of such things as drought and flood relief, insurance mechanisms, and public employment programmes. The market-based risk-adjustment options include forward trading, interlocking of factor and product markets and insurance coverage.

Communal risk-adjustment strategies refer to group-based measures that require collective decision-making either for utilizing or for preserving private or common property resources. The pooling of resources such as bullocks or implements is also part of communal risk-adjustment strategies.

Once the range of risk-adjustment options is known, households may modify their perceptions, their responses, or both by changing the discount rate or time-frame used for appraising returns from each investment. Thus while a discount rate captures the control the household has in a given resource market, the time frame may capture the certainty with which the household views a particular resource stream. In fact, either of the two can be used to derive risk preference. The shorter the time-frame in which households (or scientists) appraise their choices, the less likely it is for technology to be sustainable. Uncertainty regarding an outcome may vary among households depending upon past experiences, accumulated deficits or surpluses in the household cash flow, expectations of future returns, and complementarity between other assets and the proposed investment.

In short, the inter-temporal aspect of sustainability requires that the time-frame of the decision-maker be long term and/or the rate of discount be low. This role is often played by the public sector in an economy in which the market may not at times look beyond the present. Community/group risk-adjustment strategies may be playing this role in high-risk, low returns kinds of situations. Such mechanisms reduce the individual risk and ensure the survival of ecosystems (such as desert environments) which would not be possible in their absence.

The stakes of different social groups in the management of ecological systems vary in each resource market. If the household budget is uneven, choices will also be influenced by the status of the budget. At the aggregate level, shifts in the portfolios can be seen by differential growth rates of various species and varieties of crops, trees and livestock. Public policy at the macro and micro levels influences the portfolios through changes in access modes, assurances (through various risk-adjustment strategies) and abilities. The changes in the individual stakes in various resource systems feed back into the ecological conditions. Once the ecological conditions are modified, changes in the enterprise mix become inevitable.

Developmental Repercussions

A key objective of development, therefore, should be to enable disadvantaged households to widen their decision-making horizon and extend their time-frame. It has been suggested by Gupta that different categories of households may use different discount rates for appraising their returns in different resource markets depending upon their control over these resources. The higher the control, the longer the time-frame may be. There could be exceptions to this in the absence of public accountability and popular control, particularly in an inflationary environment (Gupta 1981). Development can be called sustainable if the management of resources, the direction of investments, the orientation of technological innovation and institutional change are harmonized and enhance both current and future potential to meet human needs and aspirations (WCED 1987). A key objective of sustainable development, therefore, should be to find incentives for short-term behaviour that are consistent with long-term goals of resource management. The excessive emphasis of various popular protest movements on improving access to resources without generating accountable and participatory institutions may result in resource degradation even after a conflict is resolved in favour of those who are disadvantaged. Long-term sustainability of short-term improvement in access may be very poor – on the other hand, evolution of sound institutions cannot take place in the absence of totally ambiguous or ill-defined rights to resources (Gupta 1989).

One reason for the failure of many natural resource management initiatives is the insistence on a standardized approach. Appropriate variability in design or organization, and options for sustainable resource use, cannot be conceptualized without an understanding of the variability of ecological endowments. This implies, for example, that farmers' adjustments to risks or the evolution of portfolios cannot be understood by concentrating on any one enterprise, such as crops, livestock, labour, or trees. The multi-institutional perspective is helpful because various resources or enterprises may be governed by various kinds of property rights regimes in combination or separately. Livestock, for instance, may be managed by some households through biomass derived only from private land. In other cases it may be derived from private as well as common and/or open access lands. Thus various institutional arrangements, whether or not regulated by the state, market or both, further influence choices at the micro-level. Any framework which ignores multi-market, multi-enterprise and multi-institutional dimensions of household portfolios provides only a partial understanding of the survival logic of people. In developing policy scenarios, especially at the national level, this should be taken into account.

3 PUBLIC POLICIES, POVERTY
AND ENVIRONMENTAL STRESS

The linkages presented in the previous chapter describe how poverty and environmental stress reinforce each other. It is the larger international and domestic policy frameworks, however, that drive and sometimes exacerbate the localized poverty-environment linkages, determine how natural resources and the environment sinks are allocated and used, and constitute the bulk of environmental problems that affect the poor. Policies may be designed to target individual producers or consumers (e.g., through special credit programmes, or food subsidies) or whole communities (e.g., literacy programmes, preventive health care). They may be designed to integrate rural and urban areas through investments in infrastructure (e.g., water supply, communications, roads) or may be designed to remove institutional barriers that block access to resources by the poor (e.g., land reform). They may also address macro-economic conditions and indirectly have substantial micro-economic, social and environmental repercussions, as is the case with structural adjustment policies.

Policies may be grouped according to whether they address problems related to the scale of resource consumption, equitable distribution or efficient allocation.

Policy Criteria

Sustainable Scale
The notion of 'scale' refers to the physical dimensions of the economy relative to the ecosystem of which it is a part and is indicated by the volume of throughput, or the flow of energy from the environment as low entropy raw materials and back to the environment as high entropy wastes. This is measured by multiplying population by per capita resource use to determine the amount of existing environmental pressure, which can then be compared to the natural capacity of the ecosystem to regenerate inputs and absorb waste outputs. The latter capacity has also been referred to as the 'space' or 'scope' for environmental utilization (the 'environmental utilization space', Opschoor 1992). In fact, this environmental utilisation space is an aggregate of the multi-dimensional claims on the biosphere that could be sustained indefinitely and thereby represents the level of the sum of environmental inputs into and outputs from socio-economic activity that the environment can 'handle' without its basic capacity in terms of functions performed for society being impaired. Scale may also be thought of as the macro-

allocation of resources, between nature and the economy as a whole. GNP may be used as an index of the scale of material throughput of economic processes. Use of non-renewable resources requires an assessment of the allocation of resources between present and future uses. This becomes a social and political question that requires an institutional perspective because future values are uncertain and do not arise from transactions between individuals.

The most important determinant of scale in developing countries is population. In developed countries scale is primarily determined by levels of resource consumption. Unwillingness to attack poverty through either population control or redistribution leaves no alternative but to trade off economic debt and/or the desire to increase material welfare for ecological debt (in the sense of claiming environmental 'space' now at the expense of environmental capital available for welfare generation in the future) through the increase of scale in resource consumption and the associated sacrifice of currently available natural capital (Opschoor 1992).

Equitable Distribution

Distribution refers to the intra- and inter-generational division of resource flow or output (per capita) among people according to ethical standards or on the basis of whether they are evenly skewed statistically. Skewed distribution of land may result from corruption, which leads to the transfer of resources to a privileged minority, and from consolidation of former subsistence and communally owned land into large private holdings dedicated to export crops. Those who remain landless as a consequence may then colonize unsuitable lands. Lack of land tenure or fear of land expropriation by the state or by powerful individuals destroys conservation incentives even on arable land. When there is a probability that policy-makers may abandon their interest in general welfare in favour of private interests then this is likely to be positively linked to the degree of economic inequality in the country. Distributional policies consist of transferring wealth through taxes and welfare payments and providing assurances of access to resources.

Inequalities of wealth and power are of crucial importance in understanding the causes and consequences of environmental degradation because they help to explain why people engage in economic activities that degrade the environment and why this should be of concern to anyone else. This is because some people reap short-term benefits from such activities while others bear the costs (Segura and Boyce 1994). Wealth is positively correlated with power, and power increases one's ability to impose negative externalities on others and to resist having them imposed on oneself. Externalities, or the non-market and uncertain environmental costs of production, are shifted to other social groups who are not parties in the transaction. These groups are thus outside or are marginal to the decision-making process, become further disenfranchised, and bear a disproportionate share of the social costs of environmental degradation caused by others.

Attempts have been made to internalize environmental costs by assigning conventional economic values to externalities. Several methodologies exist to extract implicit or explicit values for environmental services from those currently using these or those who currently feel they have a stake in maintaining them. Much progress has been made in applying such methodologies, particularly in developed countries, and to a lesser degree in developing countries, and they do appear to be useful in demonstrating the existence of values, or preferences, for environmental quality and natural assets beyond what market signals, such as prices, reflect. However, to a large degree these can still be considered arbitrary because of their uncertainty, because their implications may not be entirely perceived or because stakeholders are simply not present yet (as in the case of future generations), and because values are socially derived. Moreover, such economic values also reflect preferences as weighted by current levels of purchasing power, which implies an inherent bias against the environmental interests of the poor (unless this is corrected by applying counterbalancing but economically arbitrary weighting procedures). A broader analysis, such as an ecological approach, which seeks to identify potential long-term implications of economic decisions and prerequisites for ecological sustainability, also may not adequately address issues of social sustainability and how human needs can be met for survival in the short term. To achieve global sustainability there must therefore be an emphasis on meeting the needs of the least advantaged in society. Otherwise, sustainability in one country or for one group is only achieved at the cost of sustainability elsewhere or for others.

Efficient Allocation

Allocation refers to the division of resource flow or input among alternative product uses within the economic system; this is increasingly done through the use of market instruments. This division is thus based on relative prices that are determined by supply and demand, and it is normally treated as a technical matter. Allocation is considered most efficient when returns per dollar are equal in all economic sectors, when prices reflect the full opportunity costs and when all discounted benefits and costs are accounted for in monetary terms. In abstract, theoretical terms, an allocation is efficient or optimal if it is possible only to increase the welfare of one agent at the expense of some other agent (so-called 'Pareto optimality'). Allocation may also refer to the division of resources between the private and public sectors. Misallocation is the source of perverse economic incentives arising from inequitable distribution of wealth and power, an incomplete system of markets ('missing markets') and other types of market failure.

Export taxes, import restrictions, overvaluation of currency above market exchange rates, availability of free fuelwood, taxes, subsidies for pesticide use and use of discounting are examples of market instruments that may have effects on, for instance, whether land is cleared for export crops, or whether subsistence agriculture is displaced to marginal lands. For example, government-sponsored tax incentives led to uncontrolled deforestation for cattle ranching in the Amazon, which would otherwise have had negative rates of return. Also, tenant farming lacks conservation incentives; the availability of free fuelwood is a disincentive to forest management; and taxes on different types of cooking fuels are not designed to minimize environmental degradation (Foy and Daly 1989; Daly 1992). Allocational policies may have different costs and benefits to upland and lowland farmers, and may affect access to credit needed to invest in agricultural productivity.

As noted earlier, a case can be made for government policies to correct market failures if such actions would be more efficient and effective than leaving allocational problems to social forces and institutions (see, e.g., Opschoor and Turner 1994). Such policies may be oriented towards market-based solutions or to the restoration and/or empowerment of other social mechanisms. Frequently, however, the capability of governments effectively to address market failures in these ways is restricted by the existing structure of interest and power and by inadequate administrative machinery.

Examples of the effects of allocation policies are found in case studies done in West Java and Nigeria by Jaganathan (1989). These studies compared changes in land use from 1976 to 1986 with socio-economic data to assess the linkages between poverty, public policy and the environment and to trace causal factors. The study concluded that market factors, public investments in infrastructure (e.g., road construction) and macro-economic policies were the primary causes of changes in the use of land and water. Monetization, which accompanies the spread of the market economy, causes land and water values to appreciate, leading to the privatization or nationalization of common property rights. Markets may also cause undesirable changes in social behaviour because they are impersonal and replace non market economic systems, based on long-term reciprocity and redistribution through personal relationships, by short-term interest-driven motivations. The largest changes in land use occurred where there were improved road connections to a highway system.

The only direct link between poverty and changes in land use was found in the use of slash-and-burn agricultural techniques in abandoned estates by landless cultivators who lacked title. Jaganathan concluded that environmental degradation was caused by badly designed and poorly executed public policies that misdirected the poor. This conclusion may have a much wider relevance than just in these studies.

Relationship Between the Criteria

The sustainable scale criterion may conflict with the criterion for efficient allocation because it acts as a constraint on the maximization of present value, which is the motive for allocative efficiency. Use of time discounting, for example, creates disincentives to the sustainable harvesting of natural resources because it creates a financial interest in liquidating stock and reinvesting the proceeds elsewhere at higher interest rates. When a discount rate is applied, long-term ecological costs will count as virtually zero, even if they are included in a monetary framework. Satisfying the criteria of scale, distribution and allocation requires that pollution limits first be established according to absorption capacities based on some method (e.g., safe minimum standards, cost-benefit analysis, or carrying capacity). This is a social and political decision on the magnitude of the 'environmental utilization space', that reflects perceived ecological limits. Limited rights must then be fairly distributed according to ethical standards – which also entails social and political decisions. The market may then be used for the efficient reallocation of goods among individual uses. The process is analogous to allocating or balancing a load on a boat in which the scale limit of the load is established by a Plimsoll line. Loading even a well-balanced boat beyond the scale limit would amount to running the risk of sinking the boat (Daly 1992).

Environmental Values and Income Distribution

As was noted above, extending the market to reflect long-term ecological costs and benefits in the prices of goods and services is not a straightforward process because of the uncertainty and variability of ecological processes, and because of the limited scope of methods to elicit environmental preferences. Also, economic commensurability does not exist in isolation from social and moral values regarding the rights of other social groups, including future generations, nor from social views (whether pessimistic or optimistic) regarding future technical changes. Monetary economic values are normally arrived at through market bargaining, which relies on contemporary individual preferences and depends in part on the present distribution of income. Placing market values on environmental resources and services also requires a social perception that they exist in limited supply. Assigning market values would therefore also require that present values be assigned to future, uncertain contingencies based on the current understanding of environmental reality. Because the poor rely disproportionately on primary commodities and other resources that are not accounted for, and therefore also on ecological services that are not valued in the market sector, the generalized market system discriminates against the poor as well as against future generations.

Although the internalization of environmental costs into an ecologically extended market could have the effect of changing income distribution by raising the costs of doing business in this area, it is not sufficient because the poor are usually in positions in which they are forced to sell cheap. This is because of the unequal distribution of assets, the segmentation of world labour markets, racial discrimination, gender inequality, unequal access to education and the inability of poor people to move freely in the world. Just as poor people are forced by such conditions to sell commodities and other environmental resources cheaply, they may also be forced to accept pollution cheaply, as was pointed out by World Bank Chief Economist Lawrence Summers when he asserted that 'the economic logic behind dumping a load of toxic waste in the lowest-wage country is impeccable'. If the poor sell cheap, the environmental resources and functions that they would own when suitable ownership rights were established, are likely to reach low values once they are brought to the market, and therefore, while the results would probably be beneficial, an extended market would not necessarily be sufficient to direct the economy towards sustainability.

For example, the use of market instruments such as a carbon and energy tax as an incentive to reduce consumption does not mean that we know how to correct the market value in order to have an ecologically correct present-day value that internalizes the relevant uncertain externalities in the future. A tax is merely a technical instrument (on a level with a system of legal standards and fines, or with a system of tradable emission permits) for reaching a reduction in emissions. The reduction objective, however, must be determined outside economics, through a scientific-political debate conducted in a terrain of factual and scientific uncertainties and stakeholder politics. So the question remains how to set ecological limits to the economy, and then to force the economy to remain under such limits through policy measures that may include market instruments? In other words, there are no 'ecologically correct' prices, in the sense that they convincingly internalize all the externalities – there are only 'ecologically corrected' prices, which make a provision for environmental externalities.

It should be stressed that all existing institutions should be made use of in achieving sustainability. While it is right to say that the market cannot correct efficiently for all environmental externalities, it should nevertheless be used as far as possible. As was observed in Chapter 1, the role of markets as an institution is increasing in the wake of the trend towards globalization and the course of events in Eastern Europe. Wherever amendments for ecologically corrected prices can be made, governments should use this as a policy instrument. If the consumer is willing to pay a higher price, for example for organically cultivated crops, this revealed preference should be employed to create a 'niche' for such products in home and export markets.

Grassroots social movements against actual or threatened externalities play an important role because they perform a function at which the market fails, by raising the costs that firms (or governments) have to pay for their use of the resources or for polluting the environment. To the extent that the market externalizes the costs of natural resources and pollution, the poor, by demanding access to natural resources, may simultaneously contribute to conservation. The struggle for survival of the poor rouses them to defend access to non-market resources and, sometimes, to conserve such resources. An example in India is the Kerala fishermen who used catamarans powered by sails and who struggled against boats with petrol engines. This was in fact an ecological struggle because it proposed the exploitation of fish without the use of exhaustible fossil fuels and at a rate compatible with fish reproduction. The struggle was also consistent with the image of the sea as something sacred. Better-known examples include the Chipko movement in India, and the movement against privatization and exploitation of Amazonian resources, on behalf of the rubber tappers, led by Chico Mendes.

Such conflicts of interests regarding the use of depletable natural resources and the conservation or destruction of environmental amenities reflect conflict among value systems and provide the basis for a valuation of resources. Because the destruction of natural resources may also destroy ecosystem processes and the cultures of those who depend on those processes, this also reflects conflict between activities to be sustained over time and the meaning of sustainable development itself. Therefore, in analysing policy options for conservation and sustainable development, it is important to identify and characterize the resources or goods that are to be sustained, and the interests that they serve (NRC 1993).

Furthermore, a conscious policy of increasing consumer awareness of an enhanced and sustainable use of such resources by shifting preferences to goods and services produced from them, could raise demand and thus harness market forces to achieve fair prices to farmers which would cover the environmental costs of production (see below).

International Trade and Aid Policies

As social structures become more complex, local conditions become more and more influenced by distant processes. Local socio-ecological systems are linked to the global system through such influences as international demand and prices for commodities. Global scale changes are part of the boundary conditions which influence the internal structure and functioning of the local system and are potential sources of stress and structural change, either harmful or beneficial. In this section attention will be paid to a range of mechanisms and policies affecting the international distribution of economic activity and of income: trade and trade policies, international borrowing and structural adjustment and development assistance. The section is rounded off by some observations on global sustainability and the need to address levels and patterns of consumption in the North.

Exchange and Welfare

Trade based on the international division of labour according to differences in the endowment of the factors of production and on differences in comparative cost ratios is normally regarded as favourable for efficiency and welfare: it leads to more products and services potentially becoming available to more people, from a given stock of production factors. Moreover, free trade between countries, that is the absence of non-market constraints on trade, is assumed to enhance the volume of trade and its allocative efficiency. Hence the predominant and well-known case for trade and trade liberalization. This case will not be developed below.

Two important considerations may, however, cast doubt on this assumed relationship between trade and welfare. One has to do with fairness, the other with environment-related qualifications about the efficiency of trade as directed by market forces. The fairness problem has two aspects: (1) are market powers distributed in such a way that the benefits of trade are indeed distributed equitably or does the market mechanism provide a context of 'unequal exchange' and (2) is there fairness to future generations, or is the issue one of the sustainability of trade and the underlying division of labour. The first of these aspects is directly related to the problem of poverty; the latter can be regarded as an environmental issue, and will be discussed below, under the heading of environment and trade policy.

Unequal Exchange

It has been said that 'practical men and economic theorists have always known that trade may help some people and hurt others'. Unequal exchange is a mechanism that transfers wealth from rural to urban areas and from poor countries to rich countries. The latter aspect will be explored here. A primary characteristic of the economies of developing countries that distinguishes them from developed countries is the extent to which they rely on exports of natural resources or primary commodities to obtain foreign currencies necessary for debt servicing, imports etc. They are therefore heavily affected by falls in commodity prices because primary commodities make up a high percentage of exports – 90% in Africa and 65% in Latin America (UNDP 1992).

This export of natural capital from undeveloped countries does not contribute to sustainable development and may trigger a process of impoverishment in so far as this capital is not supplemented by, or transformed into, human and/or physical capital in those countries. Extractive activities differ fundamentally from production activities because they are located at the sources of the raw materials that are randomly distributed – usually far away from economic and demographic centres where new production facilities can take advantage of pre-existing infrastructure, labour, services and the local economic linkages through which goods are distributed, as well as continuity with existing settlement patterns. In a productive system, the unit cost of production decreases as production increases. In extractive systems it is the opposite, because as resources are exhausted, they can be obtained only from more distant sources or may be harder to extract. An extractive economy may thus impoverish both people and the environment if the materials and energy flowing out are not transformed into infrastructure and a social organization that could provide the momentum for future development. It may also result in a lack of political power and the inability to raise prices or to halt extractive activities. In some cases, such as in the boom-and-bust of the rubber industry, the low ratio of labour and capital to value initially produces a rapid rise in regional income, followed by collapse, and profits are concentrated in the exchange rather than in the extractive sector. Extractive activities may also displace existing communities, particularly indigenous communities and those who live in areas where land ownership is not legally defined.

This process is the basis for the 'unequal exchange' of extracted, non-renewable or slowly renewable 'products' (including soil nutrients) and products that are rapidly produced. For example, Mexico exports large quantities of fossil fuels at low prices to the United States, where much of this energy is used for agriculture. The United States then exports cheap cereals, which may undermine Mexican peasant agriculture. Mexican peasant agriculture, however, is more efficient than United States agriculture in terms of the amount of energy consumed for the amount of food that is produced and the value of biodiversity. If, as is proposed in NAFTA, Mexico removes barriers to imports of United States maize, this unequal exchange would also lead to genetic erosion because United States corn is a hybrid that depends on genetic resources from Mexico to maintain its resilience. Maize originated in Mexico and, as a form of cultivated natural capital, it relies on its wild and weedy relatives, a form of natural capital, and upon the human-ecological complex of each society that has managed to create, preserve and further create such a wealth of genetic resources and which is defined as cultural capital (Martinez-Alier 1993). Box 1 summarizes some aspects of the relationships between agriculture-based trade and the environment.

Exchange under such conditions may in fact result in net transfers of wealth to the North and enhance consumption there, both per capita and in absolute terms.

Additional resource consumption in the developed countries may accelerate different categories of environmental problems, such as global warming and loss of the earth's ozone layer.

Box 1: Agricultural Trade and the Environment

Debates over agricultural trade and the environment may go back at least as far as the beginning of recorded history.

The Roman Empire in the two last centuries BC saw a decline in grain farming in Italy due to cheap imports from Sicily and Egypt, with a subsequent loss of fertile land in Italy.

In 1846, when the British Parliament repealed laws regulating wheat imports that were meant to protect British farmers from sudden drops in prices, free-trade theorist Richard Cobden proclaimed that free trade would lead to a dramatic intensification of British agriculture, including 'draining, extending the length of fields, knocking down of hedgerows, clearing away trees which now shield the corn'. He went on to extol the virtues and benefits of forcing farmers to 'grub up hedges, grub up thorns, drain and ditch' (Ritchie 1993).

In more recent times, in the United States and perhaps elsewhere, farm subsidies have been used explicitly for the purpose of holding down prices in order to 'drive other exporting countries out of the world market'. Since the United States controls a large share of the world's farm commodity markets, these subsidies force other countries to lower their prices to match because they have become dependent on foreign trade. By boosting volume to make up for low prices, prices are driven even lower. By driving down crop prices, world market forces have driven 30 million farmers off the land since 1940, forcing the 5 million who are left to become increasingly dependent on toxic chemicals and giant machinery. Overcrowded cities, polluted water supplies and overburdened tax systems are just a few of the many serious by-products of this massive dislocation (Ritchie 1993).

History also provides notable examples of complex non-market trading systems that were instead designed to increase human welfare; one was in operation in the Andes Mountains of Latin America before the Spanish Conquest. Trade was a necessity because of the high variety of micro-environmental zones found in this mountain environment. This led to a 'vertical economy' based on trade among complementary environmental zones. Trade, based on principles of reciprocity and redistribution rather than on narrow market principles, also provided a mechanism for spreading the risk of crop failure and for increasing food security.

Paying fair prices to farmers that cover the full environmental costs of production is an important first step towards global sustainability, because agriculture is central to the connection between the ecosystem and the human economy. The viability of smallholder agriculture may have important ramifications throughout the rest of the economy because it employs more people both directly and indirectly, reduces incentives to migrate to urban areas, increases food security and does a better job of conserving natural resources and protecting biodiversity and environmental quality (see the section on institutions for sustainable development). Of course the argument in favour of paying fair prices is, of course, to be extended beyond the sphere of agricultural production.

Gains from trade are usually overstated because they are often obtained by shifting resources from subsistence production, which is not accounted for in markets, to export crops, which are accounted for. When land is seen as valuable for growing export crops, there are also incentives to expropriate land from subsistence farmers, who may then become 'shifted cultivators' as they migrate into marginal areas not suitable for cultivation and who are then blamed for environmental damage. If the pattern of demand for traded natural resources in rich countries encourages unsustainable management of those resources in poor countries, that pattern of demand may threaten development prospects in the future.

Market Failures

The notion of the superiority of free trade as being beneficial for all parties is based on the assumptions that there are no externalities, that prices reflect the full costs of production and are stable, that countries have equally dynamic comparative advantages, and that the factors of production are immobile. The concept of market advantage ignores externalities, and fails to consider natural capital as a factor of production and as part of a country's comparative advantage.

Initial conditions are important to future economic development because 'trade with developed nations may prevent industrialization in less developed countries', so locking a country with the least dynamic comparative advantage into 'economic stagnation and the bottom end of growing inequality'. An economy that began with low levels of human and physical capital would then remain permanently below an economy that was initially better-endowed. With factor mobility, comparative advantage becomes less relevant from the perspective of nations, because factors will flow across borders according to the logic of absolute advantage. Comparative advantage may also lead to specialization and dependence, which is a source of vulnerability. In effect, the expansion of trade has been accompanied by growing income differentials between countries, while the gains are unequally divided within some of them, and has become a vehicle of redistribution from poor to rich.

Some commentators have felt that, in addition to entering markets as unequal partners, when developing countries do have an advantage, the rules are changed. Restrictions on trade actually cost developing countries $500 billion a year, which is 10 times what is received in development assistance. These restrictions consist of tariff and non-tariff barriers designed to exclude manufacturers from developing countries, and of immigration restrictions that prevent workers from seeking higher returns for labour. Tariffs that increase with the level of processing discourage manufacturing activities that would add value to primary commodities.

On the other hand, 'global competitiveness' usually reflects not so much a real increase in resource productivity as a standards-lowering competition to reduce wages, to externalize environmental and social costs, and to export natural capital at low prices while calling it income. Failure to protect domestic industry from competitors with lower environmental standards means that only the strongest economies will be able to maintain domestic environmental protection and will be under continual siege from constituents concerned with international competitiveness (Ekins *et al.* 1995).

Environmental externalities provide ample examples of externalized or non-internalized costs that, in themselves, imply market failures. Exploitation of natural resources without taking into account the value of those resources for future users leads to a similar type of market failure. Hence the need to make trade and environment mutually supportive through international action.

Trade and Environment Policies

The Declaration of Rio, in Principle 12, calls upon states to cooperate in promoting a supportive and open international system conducive to economic growth and sustainable development. Trade measures for environmental purposes should not be a means for discrimination or trade restriction. Principle 16 calls upon national authorities *inter alia* to ensure that environmental costs be internalized in prices, without distorting international trade and investments. Agenda 21 regards international trade as the first of its (four) programme areas under the heading of 'international cooperation for sustainable development' and the mutual reinforcement of trade and environment as the second (Par. 2.3). The point of departure is that an open, fair, non-discriminatory system of multilateral trade, that is compatible with the objectives of sustainable development and that is conducive towards an optimal allocation of global production on the basis of comparative costs, is in the interests of all trading partners (Par. 2.5). In fact, the main objectives of Agenda 21 in this respect are: (1) the promotion of an open, non-discriminatory and fair trading system, (2) improved access to markets for export products from developing countries, (3) better functioning markets for commodities and resources, and (4) policies that ensure that economic growth and environmental protection are indeed mutually reinforcing (Par. 2.9). One of the proposals – especially for developing countries – is the internalization in prices of the efficient and sustainable use of the factors of production including environmental costs and resource user costs (Par. 2.14). Other activities recommended include: (1) addressing environmental issues at the source in such a manner that measures are not unfairly trade restrictive, (2) the avoidance of market distortive measures to compensate cost differences based on differences in environmental standards, (3) the participation of developing countries in multilateral agreements, for example through special transitionary arrangements, (4) improvement in the correspondence between multilateral arrangements in the areas of trade and the environment (Par. 2.22).

Ensuring that trade and environment are mutually supportive entails the internalization of environmental externalities and future resource scarcities. Problems associated with 'trade versus environment' may arise as conflicts due to the absence of a multinational regulator, conflicts over instruments and conflicts over the use of trade measures for environmental purposes (Verbruggen and Jansen 1995).

On the first of these, the principles on which trade and environmental policies are based need to be harmonized or at least be made compatible, and international cooperation needs to be extended, as is recognized in Agenda 21. The major principles governing international relations between countries are those of sovereignty and of non-intervention. In the absence of a single global authority, international agreements are the best institutional arrangement to define and regulate the transboundary effect of countries' behaviour. Both trade agreements and environmental agreements deal with exceptions to, or infringements of these principles. Trade rules regulate a country's capacity to protect its domestic industry; environmental agreements may curb countries' possibilities for shifting environmental pressures onto others or to the global commons. From a trade perspective, products and countries are the obvious entities to take into account, whereas from an ecological perspective environmental impacts on receptors (e.g., humans, ecosystems) are, and these may be related to production processes, technologies used, locations selected, etc. Trade policies are basically driven by an interest in enhancing welfare through economic growth and an efficient use of resources, which are assumed to ensue from trade liberalization. Environmental policies on the other hand, are driven by a concern over sustainability which does not coincide with efficiency, and which is sensitive to the risks of relying on liberalized markets in situations where prices do not fully reflect costs. Trade policy tends to be concerned with government failures, whereas environmental policies are concerned with market failures.

The current multilateral arrangement for trade (GATT) does not explicitly recognize the possibility of market failures and their prevalence in relation to environmental and resource problems, nor does it contain a principle to deal with such market imperfections. It is important that, in line with Principle 16 of the Rio Declaration, multilateral arrangements ensure that environmental costs be internalized, taking into account that, in principle, the polluter should pay the cost of dealing with the environmental degradation he gives rise to. Beyond this 'polluter pays' principle, which basically operates under national authorities, a user-pays principle could be developed and, to facilitate the emergence and acceptance of international environmental agreements, beneficiary/victim analogues could be brought forward and tested (e.g. joint implementation). Another principle in the Declaration of Rio may have significance for trade arrangements as well: the Precautionary Principle alluded to in Principle 15. When nations challenge other nations' environmental standards on grounds of their protective impacts, the burden of proof could be shifted from the challenged nation (as in GATT) to the challenging nation (as under NAFTA) to show that these standards are arbitrary, discriminatory or protectionist.

In the area of instruments and measures, conflicts have arisen in relation to: (1)

environmental standards and (2) trade sanctions for non-compliance with environmental agreements. In the context of sustainability-oriented policies the need has been expressed to develop internationally agreed minimum standards of environmental quality. In the long run this might be in the interest of future generations in all countries involved, but in the short run this may be felt, especially by developing countries and economies in transition, to be taking away comparative advantages they have in developing economic activities in particular sectors. In relation to trade policies the issue has arisen of the need for environmental standards to be related to products and/or production and processing methods (PPMs). Given the fact that products are the core entities in trade policies, there is a tendency to avoid PPMs; however, as we saw, from ecological motives it is important that such impact-oriented instruments become available in principle, especially when internationally agreed minimum standards of environmental quality do not materialize. Product-related environmental measures are increasingly applied in developed countries; these include standards, charges and ecolabelling based on cradle-to-grave environmental product performance. The latter may easily go beyond what is permitted by prevalent trade rules in that they may exert influence beyond the national boundaries.

Trade sanctions in environmental agreements have met with scepticism and opposition, as they are second-best approaches to environmental goals achievements. Yet, in a world of imperfect markets and prices that are distorted by the absence of effective cost internalization mechanisms, they may have a role to play, as is implicitly recognized by Agenda 21. Chapter 39 indicates that trade measures taken in relation to environmental considerations should, if necessary, adhere to the principles of non-discrimination, least trade restriction, transparency and the need to take into account the special conditions and needs of developing countries (Par. 39.3-d).

International Borrowing and Structural Adjustment

At the beginning of the 1980s the World Bank realized that its development projects quite often seemed to fail as a consequence of defective physical or administrative infrastructure or price mechanisms. Secondly, the occurrence of the international debt crisis at the beginning of the 1980s led to general doubts about the effectiveness of project financing. Developing countries faced a debt crisis in the 1980s when average lending dropped following a dramatic rise in interest rates after the second oil shock. From 1972 to 1982 lending averaged $31 billion a year, peaking at $36 billion in 1981. From 1983 to 1990 the average was $21.5 billion annually. Developing countries then increased production to pay debts, which caused commodity prices to fall. Commodity prices also fell because there was less demand, because cheaper replacements were sometimes developed, and because of the recession in industrialized countries. Poor producers were often paid less than rich producers for identical goods because they did not have financing, needed to time their sales, and were forced to sell in weak markets at distressed prices (UNDP 1992). The liquidation of debts may perpetuate the downward spiral of poverty if it cannot keep up with the fall in prices it causes. While it diminishes the number of dollars owed, it may not do so as fast as it increases the value of each dollar owed, leading to what has been called the 'great paradox and chief secret of most, if not all, great depressions: the more debtors pay, the more they owe' (Professor Irving Fisher 1933 cited in UNDP 1992). Price indices of non-fuel commodities exported by developing countries fell 50% between 1979/81 and 1988/90 because of oversupply due to productivity improvements and export subsidization in developed countries, and increased production in developing countries prompted by debt-service obligations and structural adjustment efforts (UNDP 1992).

In response to the situation sketched above, the World Bank in 1980 introduced a new type of development programme, the Structural Adjustment Programmes (SAPs). These programmes should contribute to economic growth in the medium term. In the year 1991 SAP-related financial allocations (Structural Adjustment Loans – SALs) accounted for 26% of total World Bank loans. Adjustment programmes aim at providing support to countries with macro-economic imbalances (regarding the current account, government budget and high inflation), micro-economic distortions (market rigidities, price distortions and imperfect competition) and/or weak economic and political institutions. The major policies tied to the SALs were demand reduction through cutbacks in public spending, policies designed to restrain the money supply, trade liberalization and realignment of national currency with international markets through currency devaluation to make exports more competitive and raise the cost of imports. Measures were also included to promote economic growth and efficiency through institutional reform in particular economic sectors. In the agricultural sector, SALs were used to encourage improvement of marketing systems and increase credit availability; in the manufacturing sector they focused on the removal of subsidies and increased efficiency and in the financial sector, privatization of state-owned enterprises in order to attract foreign capital. In response to public pressure, some emphasis was also given to public spending in the most vulnerable social sectors (Reed 1992).

SALs were widely criticized because they reflected short-term approaches to long-term problems, because they overlooked external conditions (such as the declining terms of trade that made it difficult to raise revenue through exports), because the focus on production for export undermined local needs and the food security of the poor, and because they increased imbalances in domestic income distribution by favouring export-oriented agricultural and industrial sectors, and marginalizing other large groups of people. The potential for economic expansion was also constrained by the reduction of public investment in infrastructure and in health and public education. Another consequence was deindustrialization following trade liberalization and the sudden reduction of import tariffs, because domestic industries were at a disadvantage in international markets. There was also resentment that decisions about major political reforms with long-term implications were being made by small groups of professionals without any public involvement. Trade and structural adjustment affect the allocation of resources between the public and private sectors, and direct the allocation of production away from domestic consumption to the export sector. This raises the cost of living for the poor, and affects the degree of environmental degradation because expansion of agricultural exports and extractive industries may require unsustainable rates of resource consumption and increase pollution.

Overall, SALs followed the old development paradigm in that they failed to define social or environmental objectives for development policy (Reed 1992).

Macro-economic stability and the removal of price distortions were assumed by the World Bank to contribute positively to environmental conservation, whereas market failures – quite often associated with ill-defined property rights over environmental goods and natural resources – and lack of environmental policy are considered to be important sources of price distortions leading to unsustainable development. As long as market imperfections and price distortions exist, substitution, technical progress and structural change are seen as difficult to realise. Moreover, macro-economic adjustment policies implemented in a situation of market and policy failures might even aggravate environmental degradation. Missing or inefficient markets would give rise to a waste of resources and lasting external environment effects, in spite of a good environmental policy. Efficient markets are expected to result in less waste of environmental resources and, provided that a good environmental policy is implemented, external environmental effects will diminish. Therefore, the World Bank therapy for sustainable development is composed of the following measures:

- removal of distortions and impediments;
- clarification of property rights over environmental goods;
- introduction of incentives for sustainable use of natural resources. Moreover, World Bank economists display a growing awareness of the environmental repercussions of macro-economic and sectoral policies, and propose that these can be mitigated or compensated for by 'complementary policies'.

Nevertheless, there has been widespread concern over the environmental repercussions of adjustment policies. One impact of structural adjustment may be that positions and initiatives gained by non-government, non-market institutions are lost. As we shall show below, these institutions play key roles in providing not only development opportunities at the local level, but also in relation to resource conservation and management. In situations of both government and market failure, these institutions have often succeeded. The advent and penetration of markets and international capital is a very pervasive development and can easily swamp the non-government, non-market institutions. There is a risk here, in that these new markets may also turn out to have deficiencies, whereas the creation of new common property rights systems is a very slow process.

Several reviews have been made of the environmental impacts of adjustment (see, e.g., Reed 1992). The first main point emerging from these reviews is that the environmental effects of stabilization and adjustment measures are mostly indirect. Secondly, they tend to be unpredictable in their direction – positive or negative – and dependent on the period that is taken into consideration. This makes it hard, if not impossible, to draw general conclusions about the environmental consequences of these programmes. Thirdly, the environmental consequences of SAPs are frequently more direct than those of stabilization. Fourthly, there is no proof that export stimulation generally implies a selling-out of natural resources. However, one cannot rule out a relationship between intervention measures and environmental effects. It seems plausible that the environmental consequences of stabilization and of structural adjustment measures differ between countries, depending on the economic structure, the 'tradables' and 'non-tradables' that are produced – including the cash and food crops that are grown – and the government policies that are pursued regarding economic, environmental and social issues etc. Much more empirical research is needed to analyse the statistical relations between specific SAPs and stabilization programmes and the net environmental pressure they entail. On the basis of the above we conclude that a good macro-economic policy may be necessary for development, but it certainly is not sufficient for sustainable development.

As a first recommendation then, we suggest that, where adjustment programmes remain macro-economic in focus, they are developed with complementary environmental programmes that, as packages, are tested for their sustainability. The World Bank has adopted the WCED definition of sustainable development: 'What matters is that the overall productivity of the accumulated capital... more than compensates for any loss from depletion of natural capital' (World Bank, 1992). This is called 'weak sustainability', since it implicitly assumes a welfare-production function with variable technical coefficients. From an ecological perspective, substitution – especially long term – is not always possible. Technical coefficients in terms of environmental, financial and human capital inputs may be fixed, at least in part. Under conditions where substitution is virtually impossible, sustainability may require that the level of environmental capital at least remains constant; this is called 'strong sustainability'. It is recommended that the World Bank take a 'strong' position with respect to irreversible losses of essential and unique environmental components and a position of 'weak sustainability' in case the substitution of natural capital for man-made capital proves viable – on the condition that the total stock of capital goods remains the same. This implies an orientation towards sustainable income growth and provides developing countries with possibilities to benefit from their natural and environmental comparative advantages. The IMF has been mandated to take into account the structural and cyclical nature of the difficulties developing countries face and the need for adjustment programmes to avoid measures with negative impacts on either national or international prosperity. In case the latter requirement is extended to welfare-threatening environmental changes, the IMF might as well consider taking a position in favour of at least 'weak sustainability'. Translation of the formal position on sustainability of the World Bank into the structures and cultures at all operational levels still needs attention.

A second major concern relates to some strategic foci that are embedded in the stabilization and adjustment programmes. Fostering unrestricted trade liberalization and unconditionally enhancing export-led growth may not always be the fastest road towards sustainable development (see also Daly and Goodland 1995). Strengthening economies by developing domestic and regional markets might be precautious and even more effective from a long-term point of view. At a more operational level, development and adjustment programmes should be evaluated according to the requirements of sustainability mentioned above. Minimum steps in that direction are: proper accounting for the consumption of natural resources in the System of National Accounts, balance of payment accounting and cost-benefit evaluations; the promotion of changes in the price structure so that labour and income become relatively cheaper and resources more expensive (see below). Also, as we shall see, changes to property rights and markets are necessary to correct for market and government failures. This involves support for and the introduction of institutions and conditions for the realization and maintenance of sustainability. Intervention measures should be tested according to their consequences for national means and possibilities regarding the realization of 'sustainability institutions'.

When a macro-economic adjustment programme is launched, it shifts the focus to growth and export at the expense of redistribution. Possible adverse environmental impacts may even be reinforced by the social repercussions of adjustment policies, unless these impacts are curbed by mitigating social and environmental policies. SAPs should have the objective of sustainable poverty alleviation and compensate for the short-term transitional costs of adjustment, including the environmental costs. Implementation of additional environmental projects might at least compensate for negative environmental consequences from intervention programmes – analogous to the 'social sector project loans'.

Another way in which the World Bank could begin to support social and environmental goals that have been democratically determined would be to insist on countries accounting for the depletion and export of natural capital. Currently the gross revenues from exploiting natural resources are treated entirely as income rather than as the sale of capital assets (Daly and Goodland 1995). As discussed in the section on natural resource accounting, this could be used to illustrate the distribution of costs and benefits and trade-offs among development strategies. It could also provide the basis for informed public participation in development policy.

A more direct instrument for gearing structural adjustment to considerations of sustainability would be for multilateral financial institutions to support a change in relative prices by shifting tax away from labour and income to throughput or material flows (including inputs such as energy as well as pollution). Public revenue raised in the conventional way is highly distortionary in that, by taxing labour and income in the face of high unemployment in nearly all countries, governments are discouraging exactly what they want more of. The present signal to firms is to shed labour, and substitute more capital and resource throughput, to the extent feasible. It might be better to economize on throughput, because of the high external costs of its associated depletion and pollution, and at the same time to use more labour because of the high social benefits associated with reducing unemployment. This would maximize the productivity of natural capital in the short run, and invest in increasing its supply in the long run. The main point, however, is that investment should be the limiting factor, and to the extent that natural capital has replaced man-made capital as the limiting factor, the World Bank's investment focus should shift correspondingly. This shift should be a key part of structural adjustment, but should be pioneered in the North (see below).

Development Assistance

Multilateral Organizations

Currently, official development assistance (ODA) is only 0.35% of the combined GNP of OECD countries, and the amount of ODA given to a particular country is usually unrelated to its poverty level. Higher levels of ODA are apparently given to countries with bigger military expenditures, and are not allocated to such priority human development concerns as education, health care, safe drinking water, nutrition (UNDP 1992). Also, since the early 1980s, as lending from private banks was reduced and as interest rates went up on old loans, the developed countries have been net recipients of funds from the developing countries, exceeding $30,000 a year since 1985 (Hancock 1989).

Critics have questioned whether there is any evidence that the poor have actually benefitted from assistance programmes. One particularly critical review (Hancock 1989) found that the primary beneficiaries of development projects were often contractors employed from donor countries, that there was a lack of accountability to the public for the manner in which aid money was spent, and that a significant portion of foreign aid budgets, possibly 35% to 50%, was spent to keep experts in the field, and on travel for official aid missions and site visits. However, these officials often spend very little time at actual sites and projects may fail simply for lack of field studies to document such factors as the appropriateness of soil conditions to the nature of a project. Projects also tended to patronize and undervalue the poor, neglected to hire local experts, overlooked successful activities by local people that reflected their indigenous knowledge of the environment, created dependency on foreign experts and were often inappropriate to local needs.

In lending for development, the emphasis has been on projects that meet the needs of the lending institutions. For example, although the mission of the World Bank is to alleviate poverty, as a bank its success is judged by the amount of loan disbursements, which are the basis for staff merit awards, rather than by the quality of the projects to which they are made. It therefore has an institutional incentive to fund large, high-profile, high technology projects such as large dams that require large loans. These types of projects often fail to achieve their objectives, and regardless of success or failure, impoverish large numbers of people who must be resettled as a result (Hancock 1989; Rich 1994).

In 1992 the World Bank approved over 200 projects, at a total cost of US$20 billion.

One of the consequences of the old development paradigm, designed to achieve economic growth for its own sake by expanding markets and seeking to modernize traditional societies, is the impoverishment of large numbers of people who are displaced as a result of large-scale development projects. These may include dams for irrigation and hydropower, transportation corridors, urban infrastructure, industrial zones and land privatization and consolidation for agricultural modernization. People may also be displaced or denied access to traditionally used lands that have been set aside as forest reserves or national parks (see Box 2).

Box 2: Development and Displacement

In some ways, displacement is the continuation of a process that began with the enclosure and privatization of the British commons in the 17th and 18th centuries, although it has accelerated in the past 30 years, especially in developing countries and related to the development process.

In addition to displacement resulting from agricultural modernization, it is estimated that 1.5 million people are being displaced by ongoing World Bank projects, and 1.5 million are threatened by projects under preparation (Rich 1994). According to one estimate, 1.2 million to 2.1 million people are displaced a year for new dam construction, and in China alone, over 10 million people were evacuated over the past 30 years for water conservancy projects.

Although the consequences vary according to individual circumstances, a common factor underlying displacement is the onset of impoverishment as a result of many factors: landlessness, homelessness, joblessness, marginalization, food insecurity and increased morbidity and mortality. Compensation, when provided, is rarely adequate, leaving farmers with smaller marginal holdings. Many are not compensated at all, because they hold only customary rather than legal title to their land, and land to which people are relocated is often unsuitable for agriculture. When the Tucurui Dam was built in Brazil, only 20.8% of 4,334 properties had formal title, and at the Sobradinho Dam, two-thirds of the properties lacked formal title. In Kenya's Kiambere Resevoir area, the average land holding of resettlers dropped from 13 to 6 hectares, livestock was reduced by more than one-third, and yields per hectare by 68% for maize and 75% for beans, while income was reduced by an average of 82%. Over one-third remained without new houses at the end of the initial period. Resettlement also increases social vulnerability because it disrupts established communities, families and kinship groups, life-sustaining informal social networks become non-functional, associations are destroyed because of the sudden departure of members and cultural identity may be lost as a result of abandoning ancestral shrines or graves and other sacred sites, and because it severs physical and psychological links to the past.

Although the World Bank has a binding internal environmental directive that requires borrowing governments to prepare and implement resettlement and rehabilitation plans for people displaced by Bank-financed projects, 'so that they are at least no worse off than before', no project has yet been identified in which this has been successfully done. This is partly the fault of local government officials, who may be reluctant to borrow for resettlement purposes and to be forthcoming about the extent of the displacement that is entailed. At other times it is the fault of incompetence and corruption. In one project, World Bank support for resettlement amounted to $63,000 per family after cost overruns of 350% but the funds were not made available to the 40,000 people who were relocated to desert-like lands that were uninhabitable in the absence of irrigation from the dam. These figures raise questions as to whether such projects would be viable if the full costs of resettlement and economic rehabilitation were included in the project costs (Rich 1994).

A central feature of development projects has been investments in physical infrastructure projects in order to provide the basis for future economic growth, although economic stagnation made it difficult for developing countries to maintain them, and they often merely increased debt burdens, in addition to being environmental disasters. But social and institutional infrastructure may be equally important because such organizations provide the structure of incentives that determine whether a project will be maintained. Development policies in the past 40 years have also destroyed and replaced traditional indigenous institutions rather than used them as the 'foundation for a social infrastructure consistent with a modern democratic political economy' (Ostrom *et al.* 1993). In an evaluation of 25 World Bank projects, deemed successful at completion, to determine if they remained economically sustainable following termination of financial and technical support, only 12 were found to be sustainable. When these 12 projects were analysed to determine the decisive factors in making each economically sustainable, the key factor shared by all was an effort to enhance institutional capacity at the design stage. More specifically, it was found that project sustainability had a correlation with the involvement of appropriate local community institutional arrangements (Ostrom *et al.* 1993).

The need for community participation in development projects has been increasingly recognized by organizations involved in development assistance in recent years and has become the cornerstone for the assistance programmes of FAO and others. A UNDP review of 55 projects in sub-Saharan Africa, in addition to finding a need for more comprehensive planning at the national level (avoiding the trend towards 'donor-driven' environmental initiatives), stressed the need for greater community participation instead of relying solely on contact with government officials. A 1992 OECD report also insists that developing country governments should 'facilitate the involvement of the intended beneficiaries through participatory approaches' (UNDP 1993).

However, it is not always clear what is meant by 'participation'. *The World Development Report*, for example, allows that 'once national priorities and policies have been set, it is often cost-effective to solve problems at the local level'. This is a very incomplete definition of inclusion. Local or community input is needed in the formulation process itself, or else those eventually in charge of implementing policy determined in a top-down fashion may find themselves trying to fit a square peg into a round hole, first because programme decisions have been made without the affected parties' valuable input, and second because the affected parties may resist a programme that was not of their own making. Other weaknesses in development will be exacerbated by the lack of opportunities for broader citizen participation in the decision-making process (Cox 1992).

Even with a sound understanding of and a willingness to facilitate participatory development, translating intentions into actions will not happen overnight, and it will not happen by magic. Full participation requires developing and implementing a methodology for identifying all the relevant actors, incorporating the needs and interests expressed by the intended beneficiaries themselves, structuring economic incentives to encourage people to participate, establishing communication, laying out procedures for joint decision-making (which necessitates reorienting bureaucratic structures organized around top-down decision-making) and mobilizing everyone involved.

These are not simple objectives, but they are not impossible to meet. One example of a large-scale project that truly attempted fully to implement a participatory strategy was the collaboration by the Mexican Government and World Bank on the Integrated Program for Rural Development (PIDER) that invested money in thousands of local poverty alleviation projects in Mexico between 1975 and 1988. PIDER systematically created and implemented a thorough yet flexible methodology for participatory development, ensuring that local citizens were consulted and that local needs were embodied in the process. While PIDER was very successful at incorporating local concerns and resources, the effectiveness and the sustainability of PIDER's projects were hampered by its failure to help build up effective local institutions (Cernea 1993). For development to succeed, such institutions must be willing and able to assist in all stages of development planning, implementation and continuation once the intensive initial assistance phase is complete (Cox 1992). Unfortunately, PIDER's experience is the norm, and the consequences have been predictable. As one evaluation of income-generating activities in Africa found, this lack of enduring structures has left 'very few successes to talk about, especially in terms of post-intervention sustainability' (UNDP 1993).

Four key approaches to participatory rural development identified by FAO are (1) to create a favourable legal and policy environment, (2) to decentralize planning and decision-making to the local level, (3) to mobilize resources for small-scale producers, and (4) to build rural people's organizations. According to FAO, this strategy enables the poor to form organizations to articulate their needs and interests and identify long-term objectives, and enables them to pool their skills and resources to achieve those objectives. In addition, autonomous rural organizations provide economy of scale that reduces the cost of delivering resources and government services to scattered small-scale producers. This in turn enables farmers to grow more food and cash crops, to generate savings that strengthen their economic base, and to acquire management, organizational and negotiating skills that can be used to further their interests. These types of projects, however, still face institutional obstacles and constraints because, according to one FAO official, 'building rural people's organizations is a long-term process' and 'participatory projects have a longer time frame than most donors are willing to accept'. Another official commented that 'the need to establish physical targets and deadlines in project documents does not fit well with participatory approaches in which people themselves should be deciding what should be done, how and when'.

In recognition of the need to coordinate their actions towards achieving sustainable development, several multilateral organizations, including UNEP, the World Bank, the Commission of the European Communities (CEC), the

International Fund for Agricultural Development (IFAD), UNDP, FAO and OAS have formed a Committee of International Development Institutions on the Environment (CIDIE). The recognition by CIDIE participants that environmental hazards must be tackled to achieve anything even remotely approaching true development, has led many members to change their policies and to adopt guidelines for environmental protection. IFAD funds an increasing number of projects in 'marginal, resource poor areas where the issues of poverty and environmental rehabilitation are closely connected'. Over 70% of IFAD projects approved since 1990 have included environmental enhancement or rehabilitation, recognizing these as an important component of rural poverty alleviation. Since 1991, all World Bank projects have been categorized according to environmental assessment – a policy that has led to the modification of several projects.

To help confront the environmental problems that impede development, over two dozen nations, together with a host of international organizations, set up a three-year pilot Global Environment Facility (GEF) in 1990 to 'address environmental problems that transcend national boundaries whose solutions provide global benefits.' Primary responsibility for implementation is shared by the World Bank, UNDP and UNEP. The GEF was established to fund those projects where the domestic costs outweigh the domestic benefits, but where global benefits outweigh the domestic cost. Projects that would be economically viable for the host country are usually ineligible. As of the beginning of 1993, 46% of the GEF's funds were committed to conserving biodiversity, 40% to the prevention of global warming, and the rest expended in global waters or ozone depletion. The GEF has added land degradation issues (especially desertification), as these issues relate to the other four areas mentioned above.

The impact and the value of the GEF in meeting its goals has, however, been questioned. Critics have pointed out that the mere existence of the GEF could potentially even hurt its own causes, as donors may feel that biodiversity or global warming is already in a sense being attended to. Others have criticized the GEF as being too 'closely dominated' by the World Bank. With over a third of its projects failing to meet their stated goals, World Bank trusteeship has come under scrutiny, especially for the lack of access for GEF personnel to larger associated loans that greatly impact on the GEF's work. Given the small size of GEF funding relative to that of even individual CIDIE organizations, in order to be effective the GEF should serve as a lever to redirect these larger financial flows towards sustainable development paths, and should be linked in some way to policy reform and capacity building (Barker 1992).

It is hard to see how these problems can be satisfactorily rectified through the GEF, given that it was set up with the understanding that no new bureaucracy would be created. In addition, while a large institution may be the appropriate tool for managing projects designed to alter energy production and consumption in order to mitigate global warming, it may be inappropriate to manage projects that would protect biodiversity – inherently small-scale, locally-oriented projects. The GEF itself has noted the difficulty in separating global from national benefits. This presents a dilemma, for the legitimacy of the GEF rests on its image as an entity dealing with distinctly global (as opposed to local) issues (Barker 1992). There is also an increasing awareness both within and outside the international development community that effective development that will combat environmental deterioration cannot be planned, implemented and sustained by actors far removed from the intended beneficiaries. Greater participation in all aspects of development is needed to make programmes more effective in their design and more efficient in their implementation.

Much of the focus of multilateral organizations is on country-level coordination and exchange of information. One large impediment to greater country-level participation is that many developing countries have yet to establish institutions to manage effectively the environment and all the intricate processes this management entails, including policy and legislation, the inclusion of environmental concerns in development, and all the necessary planning, coordination and implementation requirements (UNEP 1992). In order to address this problem, the World Bank has provided assistance to developing countries, including at least 20 African nations, to help these countries formulate National Environment Action Plans (NEAPs) to develop and implement a framework for integrating environmental considerations into policy action (UNEP 1992). The African Development Bank has identified institution building as a priority area. Actions such as these, while positive, will not in themselves rectify the problem. As UNEP points out, while identifying problems and changing policy may fairly quickly be undertaken, changing attitudes and institutions will not happen overnight. The commitment to and involvement of nationals in the design and implementation of institutions is crucial and will require developing countries to undertake some fairly broad internal changes themselves (UNDP 1992).

In developing countries, central governments are currently responsible for over 90% of total social spending. If these governments are effectively going to advocate more participatory decision-making to the international community, they will need to look inwards and decentralize some of their social and development programmes. Such decentralization would be likely to increase the efficiency of their development spending, because projects should be more selectively suited to local needs, local employment should increase, and since the community will in a sense be spending its 'own' money and residents will feel more included in the process, there will be an added incentive to lower costs and increase performance. Countries that have attempted this have had some positive results. In Indonesia, for example, decentralizing expenditure has improved basic services in health and education (UNDP 1993). Decentralization does have a potential downside. It can lead to overlapping efforts, the loss of economies of scale, poorer services from ill-equipped local authorities, and an increase in the disparity between regions and districts, especially if more services are funded locally because poorer areas have a smaller tax base (UNDP 1993). However, these legitimate concerns do not alleviate the need for developing nations to shift towards more participatory decision-making. They simply point out the potential complications that need to be addressed.

The Role of Non-governmental Organizations

NGOs have made important contributions to reaching the poor, proving themselves able to help the most disadvantaged groups, where governments have been unable or unwilling to do so, and to respond quickly to emergencies (UNDP 1993). Their familiarity with local conditions, as well as with the social, cultural and traditional aspects of the population, direct contact with local communities and grassroots groups and their ability to disseminate information places them in a position to help implement more participatory decision-making. They also bring a different perspective from the multilateral organizations and have made important contributions to sustainable development activities. A CIDIE poll of its members showed that the contributions of NGOs are increasingly valued in sustainable development activities. The international community also has realized the need to include NGOs at all levels of development. The GEF, for example, has created a GEF/NGO Task Force, perhaps signalling a shift towards working through local NGOs on small-scale, community-based projects (Barker 1992). Several CIDIE members, including IFAD, encourage or even require NGO and public participation in the Environmental Impact Assessment process.

Local Organizations

Including NGOs in the process of development is but one step in a more participatory approach. Programmes must 'engage everyone affected, particularly the beneficiaries, to such a degree that they will choose to remain involved over time'. Unless this is done at the design stage, programmes are likely to meet resistance, requiring coercion, or at the least large subsidies to continue, and may be of questionable benefit to the community. Top-down formulation may make for an easier policy-making stage (fewer actors, narrower ranges of options, etc.), but may spell disaster in the implementation stage. Any stakeholders who could hinder programme implementation need to be included in the formulation stage.

The international development community has recognized this need. Recent UNEP publications have stressed that the problem-solving process should inform and bring together stakeholders to negotiate a solution. Resource problems require the mobilization of all of societies' participants. Community participation is essential both in making sound decisions and in ensuring that the community will support a project once it is undertaken. The Chairman of the GEF has stressed the need, especially in developing countries, to 'bring a wider range of organizations into the process, particularly at the grassroots'. FAO actively seeks to broaden the role of communities and public participation in its decision-making structure.

Though perhaps rare, effective local institutions have been created. The Coordinating Body of Indigenous Peoples' Organizations of the Amazon Basin (COICA), for instance, represents 1.2 million members of some 327 different indigenous groups spread over nine Amazon Basin countries. Founded in 1984 with help from multilateral organizations, COICA has developed territorial defence strategies, concentrating on obtaining legal title. In 1990, representatives from 271 Northern organizations met with COICA, thus formalizing an indigenous-environmentalist alliance.

Another local organization, CICOL in Bolivia, works with indigenous communities to develop sustainable forest management, and encourages the processing of lumber at indigenously controlled mills (Oxfam 1993b). Building up local institutions of indigenous peoples is necessary not only to secure their future, but probably even that of the rainforest – and COICA and CICOL are strong examples of how institution-building can help reverse the downward spiral of the poverty-environment linkages.

The success of CICOL may shed some light on the concept of debt-for-nature swaps. Often formulated with less than the full input of all the actors, these may unwittingly trade away the land rights of indigenous peoples and are sometimes ineffective in preventing deforestation or squatting. Protecting land by keeping people off has proven inadequate, given economic and population pressures. Perhaps a better alternative, and an excellent example of including locals in the process fully, are debt-for-indigenous stewardship swaps, which allow indigenous peoples to remain on the land. As these peoples depend on the forest for survival, they have a life-or-death interest in maintaining the forests, and thus act as effective built-in protection. Similar debt-for-sustainable-development swaps have even been suggested by UNEP as an innovative approach the CIDIE should take in order to meet Agenda 21 (UNEP 1992).

Long-term, sustainable environmental management also requires broad-based approaches to human development. Education is one seemingly independent variable that is actually tied into the linkage dilemma. For example, CEDNA is an independent development agency that has worked with the Quechua Indians of Bolivia, starting a bilingual newspaper, a Quechua-language radio station, and generally working to increase literacy and education levels. Basic education has expanded into environmental restoration, and reforestation and soil conservation techniques have spread. Small-scale lending programmes are another avenue for enabling people to extricate themselves from the poverty trap. Some of these programmes have proved to be remarkably efficient, both in opening up access to capital for those previously denied it, and the effectiveness of the investment. One of the biggest success stories has been the Grameen or 'Village' Bank. Starting with the assumption that if given access to credit the poor would prove themselves 'bankable' and productive, and would be able to move themselves out of poverty, Mohammad Yunus, a United States-trained Bangladeshi academic, began personally guaranteeing bank loans in 1976. By 1983 the project had become a bank. The procedure is elegantly simple. Individuals desiring a loan are required to band together in groups of four or five, with each member of the group guaranteeing repayment of a loan made to any other. Thus the group acts as a form of alternative collateral, providing support and powerful peer pressure.

The Bank is a very decentralized institution, staffed by so-called 'bicycle bankers' who carefully select borrowers, and rigorously supervise and monitor the projects. This local selection and oversight has helped the Bank to succeed and to become self-sustaining, with repayment rates reaching 97%. Loaning out roughly $25 million a month, the Bank has had an enormous effect on its more than 1.6 million. Only 20% of Bank members live below the poverty line, far below the usual figure of over 50% for their counterparts who are not members. One study found that Grameen members earned 43% more than corresponding members of their communities. The programme has reached out especially to poor rural women, who, as Yunus said, 'see the worst kind of poverty'. Also, women are more likely to put their earnings into family nutrition, health and education. As of 1993 women made up 93% of the Bank's borrowers.

Governments can institute effective small-scale lending programmes as well. Chile has instituted a national lending programme that has been a large factor in helping an estimated 15–20% of its population escape from poverty over the last three years. Small businesses that make up the informal economy and that normally have no access to capital, employ roughly 40% of the work force and 80% of the very poorest segment of the workforce. The government has contracted with Chilean banks and NGOs to provide small loans to these so-called 'microentrepeneurs', offsetting the proportionately large transaction costs incurred in processing loans of such small amounts. In a similar programme, members of private associations work with small companies, helping to develop an investment plan. The organization then acts as a conduit between the company and a bank, and helps supervise the loan. Both of these programmes have been very successful, putting people to work, expanding production and raising people out of poverty. Repayment rates have been above those of traditional commercial loans.

An Institutional Approach towards Development

The review given above suggests that increasing aid along traditional channels is unlikely to lead to significantly better and more efficient results. Large, complex development plans governed by fixed goals and requirements allow little flexibility or adaptability. These may work in developed nations, where conditions are fairly predictable, but not in developing countries, where unpredictability is, in a sense, almost the only predictable thing (Cox 1992). For development to be successful, projects need feedback, and the ability not just to monitor results according to predesigned standards, but to respond and adapt to the situation at hand. Emphasis needs to be given to developing local institutions and to endowing individuals with the skills to continue and sustain the development process. Debate and dialogue between all the parties involved need to be increased. Stakeholders need to adopt a more 'result-oriented' system, shifting to a more field-based approach that incorporates the beneficiary community's feedback instead of simply trying to follow the original agenda (Cox 1992).

Greater participation from all parties with an interest in the programme or business – environmentalists, community organizations, government, and the beneficiaries themselves – may be a necessary condition for success. Unfortunately, while the concept of participation has been affirmed, few countries or development agencies have undertaken these types of small-scale, participatory, community-oriented projects, focusing on the more macro-policy initiatives (Durning 1989). The time required for the necessarily slow gradual implementation that participatory projects require is unfortunately much longer than the time-frame within which governments and large organizations normally work. But even if those in control are willing to change, and even though analysts have called the proliferation of community-based self-help groups 'the most heartening trend on the poverty front', there is a potential dilemma (Durning1989). Though working with community-based organizations on highly participatory projects may be much more efficient and much more effective than traditional development efforts, these small-scale projects are just that – small – and they do not have enough impact to pull whole populations out of the poverty and environment trap. For example, though the Costa Rican Fundación Costarricense de Desarrollo provides extensive credit to the poor, its considerable effort still only constitutes 0.2% of total credit.

Even the above noted Grameen Bank in Bangladesh only accounts for 0.1% of national credit (UNDP 1993).

This dilemma may be avoidable. Although decreasing returns in relation to scale may set in as the scope of a project increases, the number of such projects may still be expanded effectively and efficiently provided each project remains small. And even if there would also be decreasing returns from a growing number of small scale projects, a shift of some of the effort and huge resources expended by international organizations and governments into participatory development may nonetheless produce large benefits. As these projects appear to be so much more effective and efficient, a slight decline in quality as the quantity increases may not offset their large initial advantage. And, as increased participation expands the resource base available to a particular project, even small investments may reap disproportionate benefits.

These small organizations may not have enough impact to move whole populations out of the poverty and environment trap, the existence of a number of small organizations may be the only appropriate management strategy in some situations, in particular those related to environmental degradation. Whereas conceptualization has to be at the national levels, execution should be planned at local levels through participatory agencies. Such an approach is now also being adopted in such areas as population planning (Srinivasan 1993; Basu 1994). The key to successful developmental planning lies in finding how national governments and local participatory organizations can best coordinate their efforts. National governments may be required to play enabling roles in a number of situations (Chopra *et al.*1990). One case in India involved the experiment of Joint Forest Management, in which formalization was at state level through the acceptance of government resolutions concerning property rights structures. Though the different resolutions passed in this context have lacunae and need improvement, in sum they have resulted in an increase to 1.5 million hectares of land coming under different forms of joint management (Ministry of Environment and Forests, India 1994).

The emergence of community managed self-help groups has been widespread, for example in Latin America and India. WWF has produced a document listing NGOs in different developmental areas in India. It appears that in land and water management alone (an area that can be considered to represent the form of environmental degradation of most significance to developing countries), more than 2,000 NGOs were working in the late 1980s or the early 1990s.

Even if small-scale programmes do not have a significant impact on society as a whole, successful programmes will nonetheless serve as examples and models for governments and development agencies to incorporate into large-scale policy initiatives. The Grameen Bank, for example, has been used by IFAD as the basis for programmes throughout the world, and 40 funds in the United States alone have been similarly patterned (IFAD 1992). President Clinton has used this Bank as the paradigm for a $382 million proposal to expand lending in poor inner city and rural areas. And the benefit these types of programmes will bring to those who are lifted out of the poverty and environment trap cannot be discounted.

Sustainable participatory institutions are a prerequisite for environmentally sustainable patterns of development and resource use. Often by their mere existence and history, traditional institutions can be seen to have contributed to such sustainable patterns of development. For several reasons, however, the existence of many traditional institutions is threatened, and the causes must be understood if the resurgence of participatory non-governmental institutions is to be successful. Traditional institutions may break down because of: (1) the intervention of market forces, and (2) the replacement of long-term reciprocity principles by those of the receipt/payment of a specific package of goods/services/money in short-term exchanges (as we shall see in more detail below). Factors favouring the re-emergence of such institutions, or more appropriate modern forms, may be divided into (1) those linked with management, and (2) those emerging from the the structure of the social and economic system. We shall address both these categories in turn.

Most of the literature on participation in resource management is about generating incentives for people to participate in externally designed programmes and projects. Even when consultation is at the design stage, the control over resources and the way these are to be used is almost always in the hands of outsiders. An alternative approach might be to begin instead with research to find out what a particular village has done collectively, without outsiders' help. In a project that did this, it was found, for example, that villagers had used a rotating and saving association or a club to generate discount money in order to buy such things as a public address system or school mats and furniture. It is this spirit of self-reliance that provides the basis for local development. Institutions that endorse cooperation and empower collective action must evolve to make collective survival possible. An organization evolves into an institution when the workers behave in the collective interest in response to internal commands rather than reacting to external demands made by that organization.

International developmental organizations are, in a sense, a third tier of development management institutions, with grassroots organizations and national governments constituting the other two. The overall challenge is to evolve structures for development that are able to coordinate effectively these three tiers. Within this setting, the challenge for development organizations is to see themselves as participants in governmental development efforts as well as to find ways to liaise with and reinforce grassroots efforts, and thus to be a link between local and global systems. What is needed is a multi-scale implementation of the basic principles that make grassroots projects work – stakeholder involvement in defining goals combined with realistic assessments of what is possible. Sustainable development can only be done in the context of accountable and responsive organizational arrangements. Self-reliance is only possible when the visions and concerns of local people are articulated in the discourse. Unfortunately, the language of discourse is alien to the idiom used at the grassroots level. Our inability to use this idiom stems partly from our reliance on English language references and terms, and partly on our insistence on looking for global, general solutions to local problems. Box 3 summarizes some principles that can provide the basis for development agencies constructively to participate in grassroots efforts to develop sustainable institutions for natural resource management (Gupta 1993).

An example of these concepts in action is provided by the 'Honeybee' network. This is a global network in which scientists collaborate with farmers to document innovative practices, primarily from dry regions. A database has been created with over 1,400 entries, which shows that although disadvantaged people may lack economic resources, they may be rich in knowledge. For example, many plant-derived drugs are used for the same purpose as were the plants originally discovered. Also, local soil classification systems may be much more elaborate than official classification systems. Vermiculture has been successful in reducing the use of fertilizer and pesticides (Gupta 1993). This network is called the Honeybee because, when bees extract honey, they greatly increase the flowers' success and adaptability through pollination. Researchers have often instead extracted knowledge from people without providing anything in return. Efforts are seldom made to connect farmers with other farmers. Use of the English language may connect researchers globally but not the people they have learned from. Researchers grow in their careers by achieving recognition, while the people continue to suffer in silence.

Some of the principles of the Honeybee network are:
- to build upon the ability of people to solve problems rather than just to articulate them;
- to maintain communication in the local language, which ensures that accountability towards people is empirically demonstrated;
- to build upon what is already known, which generates the right context for authentic learning.

An example of a business founded upon similar principles is Shaman Pharmaceuticals. This is a company that works in partnership with indigenous communities to discover and develop novel pharmaceuticals from plants with antifungal, antiviral and sedative/analgesic properties, in order to develop sustainable harvesting methods that benefit local economies and conserve genetic diversity of the species, and to provide reciprocal benefits to communities which have indigenous ecological knowledge. Plants are identified for screening through interaction between practitioners of ethnobotany and Western medicine, and members of indigenous communities. In the 50% of samples screened for these properties, 74% correlated with their original ethnobotanical use. Particular attention is being paid to plants obtained from secondary forest habitats because, as pioneer species, they are more suitable for sustainable harvesting. In order to provide reciprocal benefits to the communities, a non-profit making organization, 'The Healing Forest Conservancy', was established to distribute profits to appropriate organizations in countries that contribute to these activities in order to develop effective conservation programmes, facilitate sustainable production and marketing of rainforest products, produce multilingual publications for use among indigenous communities, and provide accurate scientific information to the conservation community regarding endangered habitats, species and populations of plants that are or may be important sources of medicine (King 1992).

Box 3: Guidelines and Principles for Developmental Agencies to Participate in Grassroots Efforts towards Sustainability

1 Building Upon What is Known Common, indigenous knowledge is important as a catalyst for social action. Experimentation and innovation may be a matter of life or death for the masses in rural areas, given the uncertainties of nature in their fragile environments. Mechanisms for sharing knowledge can enable individuals to collaborate by pooling expertise and directing efforts where they are most needed.

2 A Successful Strategy Self-destructs A project is successful when it becomes unnecessary, because it has solved the problem it was designed to address. A project is sustainable when it can continue to function without external support. Organizations designed to solve certain problems may have vested interests in keeping the problems alive to avoid becoming redundant. Governments preferably have an enabling versus provisioning role. Institutions must be designed so that they can self-destruct when they have achieved their goals (Gupta 1993).

3 Building on the Self-Design and Learning Potential of Development Organizations 'Eco-specific planning' requires a wide range of organization designs, policy content and delivery systems. Centralized monitoring systems concentrate on uniform standard indicators and reinforce risk-aversion compliant behaviour by functionaries in organizations. The insistence on standard indicators not only curbs creativity but also prevents organizational adaptation to ecological diversity. The accountability to people having cultural diversity, which is necessary for maintaining ecological diversity, can be measured by the amount of latitude for creative deviance permitted in the developmental organizations (Gupta 1993).

4 Sustainability of Spirit A key dimension of sustainability is the need for the spirit of sustainability. Unfold locked-up entrepreneurial energy and the creativity of all those involved. The momentum so generated may eventually solve the problem. The spirit of sustainability is prior, the substance is subsequent (Gupta 1993).

Underlying social and economic structures have a crucial impact on the sustainability of newly emerging institutions. The evolutionary process, as a consequence of which participatory institutions get established, may be triggered by the emergence of leadership of an extraordinary calibre. Alternatively, an exogenously developed institution (embodying the principles of participation) could be introduced in a village economy as a consequence of similar evolution in nearby areas. The origin, replication and sustenance of participation can be traced to: (1) the nature of links between privately owned property (PPRs) and common property resources (CPRs), (2) the possibilities of economies of scale, and (3) the distributional rules and arrangements (Chopra and Kadekodi 1991).

Links between PPRs and CPRs Where private resources (such as land and livestock) are more equitably distributed, most people will also need CPRs (such as pasture land and forests and irrigation water) as inputs into private production. This complementarity will ensure the minimization of conflict in the sharing of benefits from conservation. In such a situation, an economy may more easily emerge from the poverty-degradation trap with the help of participatory institutions.

When PPR ownership is concentrated in a few households, only they may participate in conserving the CPR primarily to reinforce the existing structure of income generation. Participation by the majority may not take place at all in the village economy. Development, with people's participation, may, however, still take place if a fair distribution of consumption benefits is made possible by rules set up by the society.

Possibility of Scale Economies Pooling of low productivity, or unproductive or degraded land economies of scale, will form the basis of participation. Consequently, common resources can be created on the pooled land and be the basis of higher levels of productivity. The crucial factor here is the availability of land and the magnitude of the scale advantage as viewed by the participants.

Distribution of Benefits Sustenance of participatory institutions will depend on the rules for distribution. Though complete equality is not a necessary condition, rules should be percieved as fair by the majority of the group.

The Role of Women in Sustainable Development

As is mentioned throughout this report, women suffer from the most pervasive disparity in access to resources. They are primary resource users and bear most of the responsibility for growing and collecting food, medicines, fuel, housing materials, providing cash income for schooling, health care and other family needs. As such, they do much of the work needed to maintain or restore the environment. As with nature, the value of women's labour is mostly outside the market and constitutes an economic subsidy. Because of the nature of their responsibilities and direct dependence on land-based resources, they are also the hardest hit by desertification, deforestation and misguided economic and development policies. As a result, they may also be agents of environmental degradation. For example, for many women, the sale of legally and illegally collected fuelwood may be the sole means of livelihood. Because in many countries they are denied the right to own property and the opportunity to receive an education, female-headed households are more likely to be found in marginal land areas (Abramovitz and Nichols 1992; Rodda 1991).

Women can have an enormous impact on conservation because of their multiple roles. Their special knowledge of the environment is derived from growing food, collecting fodder, gathering firewood and water, caring for children, the sick and the elderly, tending domestic animals and gathering medicines. Communities may depend on diverse products, from a wide area over different seasons, to provide a resilient economy. In some African villages women may keep as many as 120 plant and animal species alive in the interstices between mechanically cultivated cash crops in fields from which they have been excluded. Often they are unable to obtain legal access to anything outside these interstices, fence rows and abandoned lands. Typical land-use surveys identify cash crops only, rather than those important to women and families. These conditions tend to divide rather than integrate home, habitat and workplace. (Abramovitz and Nichols 1992).

In Africa, 70% of food crops are grown by women, in Asia 50-60%, in Latin America, 30%. Women are also usually responsible for marketing agricultural produce. In Africa they do up to three-quarters of all agricultural work in addition to domestic responsibilities. These responsibilities and workloads have increased as men have left home to work in the towns, in mines or on plantations. Even where women have more responsibilities for cash cropping, but still do not usually have land rights, decisions about land-use changes continue to be made by men, who also have access to credit, training and new technology. As wage labourers, women are usually employed in the most labour-intensive tasks such as coffee-picking, pesticide spraying without protective equipment, and labour-intensive manufacturing jobs in export processing for transnational corporations (Rodda 1991).

Discrimination may begin at birth, when girls are valued less than boys, and they may as a consequence receive less nutrition and medical attention. Their health may be further undermined by marrying at a young age and bearing children too early and too often. Although many women would prefer fewer children, they have to travel great distances to obtain contraception, and need acceptance of it by men. Overall, 60% of the population of developing countries has easy access to contraception – based on whether its cost will entail the equivalent of more than two hours a month and no more than 1% of wages, but there is wide disparity. This level of access is 95% in East Asia, 57% in Southeast Asia and Latin America, 54% in South Asia, 13-25% in Muslim countries, and 9% in sub-Saharan Africa (Rodda 1991).

Because of their multiple roles, women are increasingly also acting as positive agents of change and have taken leadership roles in environmental conservation. For example, it was primarily women who initiated the well-known Chipko Movement in India that prevented the destruction of large forest areas through non-violent resistance. They have also been involved in tree planting efforts, such as the Green Belt Movement in Kenya to prevent the spread of desertification, in introducing conservation practices, such as terracing and reafforestation in Honduras, and in other projects aimed at preventing erosion, providing fuelwood, clean water and sanitation, and the use of ecologically sound agricultural practices, as well as in developing skills in resource management and improving standards of living. In urban slum areas, women have also taken the lead in clearing dumps and in organizing savings for housing funds. Formation of credit groups is also helping to increase womens' access to resources and training (Rodda 1991).

In order to be effective, women must gain more control of resources and of development planning, rather than participating in mere 'involvement'. Their needs and roles must also be integrated into decision-making in general rather than being treated separately by being confined to a 'women-in-development ghetto' where they may be given low priority. Just as for all human beings, technologies should be designed to meet their needs rather than to displace them (Abramovitz and Nichols 1992).

Addressing Levels and Patterns of Consumption

The two sources of environmental degradation distinguished earlier in this chapter, i.e. unsustainable development in the developed countries and impoverishment in the undeveloped countries, are linked: they are both the result of global patterns of economic growth and trade (Gallopin 1989). Cumulatively, their effects diminish the earth's capacity to support life and threaten global security.

Sustainable development is a concern for which countries have a common, but differentiated responsibility. Several initial steps towards it must first be achieved in the North. In other words, trade adjustment and aid policies themselves are insufficient to ensure sustainable development at the global level. It is unrealistic to expect any sacrifice for the maintenance of sustainability in the South if similar measures have not first been taken in the North. The major weakness in the ability of most multilateral institutions to foster environmentally sustainable development is that they have leverage only over the South, not the North. Some way must be found to push the North also.

Several issues should be treated as the special responsibility of developed countries. They should take the lead in 'merging environment and decision-making' in both national accounting and in internalizing environmental costs, and they should consider and address the consequences of their life-styles and consumption patterns on global sustainability. Some countries (e.g., the Nordic countries and the Netherlands) have already begun to do this. Accounting systems will be discussed below; internalizing environmental costs in market prices through direct regulations and economic incentives is a general phenomenon in OECD countries (Opschoor *et al.* 1994). Discussion on shifting the tax base from labour and income to environmental inputs and outputs has started (e.g., the energy/carbon tax in Europe) question, and the issue of consumption and production patterns has been put on the agenda of OECD.

Legal and Property Rights Structures

The structure of property rights can act as a powerful constraint on the sustainable management of resources and influence choices about land use because they can provide assurances of future access and predictability about the behaviour of others. The land rights of indigenous farmers have usually not been recognized because they were regarded as having only customary 'communal' rights to land rather than legal entitlement and permanent rights that could be leased, sold or inherited (Netting 1993). States could then declare ownership and collect taxes as rent for its use. As market values increased, subsistence agriculture was often displaced in favour of commercial agriculture producing crops destined for export. In Brazil, the extensive rural out-migration of the past several decades coincided with the timing of agricultural modernization and was most intense in agriculturally developed areas. Overall, in Brazil, it has been estimated that 28.4 million people were displaced between 1960 and 1980 by export-oriented agricultural modernization intended to earn foreign exchange (Rich 1994).

Establishment of legal title in 'top-down governmental land-registry schemes' was just as bad because these ignored customary and actual land uses, and often discriminated against women by granting land titles to men. They also attempted to consolidate scattered plots, and were generally rigid, arbitrary and subject to corrupt adjudication favouring outsiders. According to progress reports on a programme of action agreed upon at the World Conference on Agrarian Reform and Rural Development held in 1979, attempts to redistribute land without a preceding restructuring of power relations achieved limited success because pre-reform land distribution generally reflected the power structure within a country, and land distribution programmes usually met with strong political resistance (FAO 1993).

In Latin America, the major beneficiaries of land-reform legislation were medium-sized farmers within the modern agricultural sector. The poorest groups benefitted less than had been hoped (FAO 1993). Practitioners of traditional agriculture in the Andes, for example, deliberately cultivate scattered plots in order to spread the risk of crop failure and to take advantage of different altitudinal zones. These traditional land uses have been routinely ignored in land-reform efforts undertaken at various times by the Peruvian government, which was motivated by the desire to consolidate these plots into single, commercially viable units.

Land in sub-Saharan Africa is mostly in common property regimes, partly because of the absence of markets for scarce resources. It has been argued that this 'institutional distortion' is responsible for environmental degradation and that markets and liberalization are necessary to conserve biodiversity. Rural households may be seen, however, as minimizing risks to survival rather than as maximizing profits. For example, cash crops on specific parcels of land are more vulnerable to poor rainfall and have a higher risk of failure. Risk aversion in production and consumption decisions is an increasing function of poverty and will lead to conservative choices under conditions of uncertainty. This may involve a commitment to an overall package in exchange for the benefits of a well-defined group of products and set of social relations.

Maintenance of traditional social systems during periods of population growth increases environmental pressure because the land becomes parcelled in sub-optimal-sized holdings, going to those with ancestral rights rather than being distributed on the basis of use requirements, and encourages over-utilization and inefficient use. Although such an institution may seem irrational because it is predisposed to degrade the environment, it may be rational for purposes of assuring social sustainability, which is also necessary for survival. Social sustainability is defined as the ability of human institutions to adapt and continue in the face of stress and shock. Such institutions are composed of individuals organized into kinship groups, communities, nations and other loosely associated subsystems that provide social flexibility and resilience (Githingi and Perrings 1993).

In Kenya, for example, overgrazing has been attributed to traditional land tenure and methods of production. Grazing practices may have been sustainable, however, prior to the alienation of traditional pasture lands by the colonial government, and the subsequent formation of individual and group ranches. The designated group ranches were not ecologically viable units and did not straddle wet and dry season grazing. Individually owned herds were often kept on communal property, and exceeded carrying capacity but were insufficient for family subsistence (Githingi and Perrings 1993).

Policy, therefore, should directly address needs that have been satisfied by institutions, in this case the income security of rural households. Adjustments should be consistent with self-organization of the system and the culture and traditions of the society to avoid catastrophic institutional change or extinction. In a study of Botswana and Kenya, Githingi and Perrings (1993) found that traditional institutions to assure sustainability disappeared or weakened, while replacement institutions failed to exercise authority. The replacement institutions in these cases attempted to recreate some aspects of those that had collapsed. These needs can be addressed through education, increasing technical skills, challenging unsustainable practices, incorporating traditional knowledge without encouraging unsustainable practices, and providing services of equal value to those offered by unsustainable institutions (Githingi and Perrings 1993).

Traditional human communities typically have developed mechanisms of collective action to solve common property resource management problems. These mechanisms are based on an understanding of the patterns of variability in resource availability which have developed in cultures directly dependent on those resources for their survival, on a recognition of the need for short-term restraint during critical periods of ecological transition, such as when fish are spawning, and on long-term reciprocity in human relationships. Economies governed by principles of long-term reciprocity and redistribution reduce the risks inherent in ecological variability and provide for cultural continuity.

Many of these mechanisms have broken down as a result of the enclosure of the commons in privatization and land consolidation schemes that have forced large numbers of people into marginal land areas. Conflicts between individual and community interests in the absence of institutional mechanisms for cooperation in the management of common property resources may lead to what has become commonly known as the 'tragedy of the commons', or less commonly, as the 'tragedy of enclosures'. Deforestation in the Amazon, for example, is the result of one of the most massive processes of privatization of land in human history (Martinez-Alier 1991). In the Brazilian Amazon, the driving forces and main beneficiaries of deforestation have been generals, land speculators and large-scale cattle ranchers. The principal victims are the 200,000 indigenous people of the Amazon, and the 2 million other Brazilians who earn their livings by gathering rubber, nuts, resins, palm products, and medicines from the forest (Guppy 1984; Hecht and Cockburn 1990). Although poor people were often employed to clear the land, sometimes in exchange for permission to grow crops for a few years before the land was converted to pasture, blaming them for destroying the forest is like blaming poor conscripts for the ravages of war.

Community Control and Management of Common Property Resources

In addition to structuring land tenure arrangements, common property resource management systems can provide an institutional framework for internalizing externalities and for recognizing poor people as stakeholders. The pooling of resources is a necessity for communities that depend primarily on natural resources (with their inherent uncertainties), because the cost of alternative maintenance of inventories is very high. Collective action is also useful as a strategy for absorbing risk. For example, common seed and germplasm reserves may be the only way to provide location-specific seed material in drought years, when farmers have been forced to consume their seeds.

Sustainable practices and technologies usually require group action or may at least be more efficient as a result of it. For example, collective action can be used to reduce the use of pesticides by monitoring for and treating hotspots and to synchronize planting in order to avoid the build-up of pest populations. Cropping systems could be managed on a watershed basis through collective action.

Common property institutions could also enable small rural enterprises to afford pollution control equipment by using common effluent treatment plants. In India, for example, the main exports are textiles and leather. The associated manufacture of dyes and chemicals are among the most polluting industries and are moving from Europe to South Asia. The environmental costs are not accounted for in the consumer price. Small-scale printed textiles plants are concentrated in the arid regions of India. Fluids from dyes and bleaching agents go into shallow streams. In Jodpur, 60% of the hand pumps provide water that is unsafe for human consumption because they have shallow bores reaching water that is polluted by textile dyes that remain near the surface because drainage is poor.

Global Environmental and Natural Resource Agreements

A common property framework could also be used as the basis for restructuring international agreements in order to correct inequities in access to globally shared resources. The debate about responsibility for reduction in CO_2 emissions, for example, illustrates how inequalities in income distribution influence the values placed on environmental functions. The rich countries saw the CO_2 absorption or 'sink' function of the oceans and new vegetation as basically free and available on a first come, first served basis. Some advocates for the poor argued instead for recognition that the ownership rights to this CO_2 sink function should be shared equally by all humankind, in such a way that poor people making little use of it (because of their low CO_2 emissions) could sell their unused part to the rich. They advocated an agreement between countries based on emissions per person, rather than open access. Since this does not impose a penalty on population growth, CO_2 emission quotas could be pegged to current population levels, which could also provide an incentive for reducing population (Martinez-Alier 1993).

If CO_2 emissions per person were brought down to the aggregate level that equals the sink function, most members of the human race would still be under their allowance. In estimates based on an index that allocates CO_2 and methane emissions to each country in proportion to its population, and calculates each country's excess emissions, the contribution of net greenhouse gases to the atmosphere of one American is equal to that of 8,150 Indians. Overall, developed countries are responsible for 70% of total CO_2 emissions, 77% of cumulative emissions from 1950 to 1988, and an average of 7 times per capita emissions. If the population stopped growing and everyone consumed as much as the United States, atmospheric carbon would double in 30 years (Agarwal and Narain 1991). From the perspective of poor people, the excess emissions of CO_2 by rich countries may be regarded as an ecological debt from the rich to the poor because they narrow the development options of the poor. Income transfers from North to South on the basis of excess CO_2 emissions could, 'move the North-South debate from the concepts of present-day aid and charity toward true international cooperation' based on 'mutual respect and dignity' in a way that recognizes 'the correct and legitimate share of the planetary resources that belong to all'.

Natural Resources and Environmental Management Policy

Historically, resources have been managed individually, for particular purposes, and to serve specific interests, without considering how they are linked in the ecosystem, and the distributional effects on other stakeholders. For example, forests have been managed to maximize timber, without considering the effects of forestry on fisheries and their role in regulating water flow, providing habitat for wildlife, maintaining biodiversity and providing non-timber resources to people. In fact, the task before most governments is to evolve a policy that balances between the different functions of forests, i.e. preserving biodiversity, serving as providers of raw materials to industry, providing livelihoods to people living in them, etc. Methodologies should be developed that enable decision-making to take into account this multifunctionality of resources and that is based on appropriate knowledge of these functions in particular economies. This is one area where Natural Resource Accounting, if properly designed, may play a crucial part (see below).

By reducing ecosystem variability, current practices may also be reducing ecosystem resilience and may produce unintended consequences, as well as increased social and economic dependence on particular resources and more rigid and less responsive resource management institutions. Some examples include: reducing insect populations with pesticides, reducing the incidence of fire through fire detection and suppression and grazing cattle with modern rangeland practices. As a result, forest architecture may become more uniform and fuel may accumulate, leading to more intense outbreaks of pests and more destructive fires. Rangeland would lose drought-resistant grasses if they lost out to more productive but drought-sensitive grasses. Reduction of mosquitoes has allowed more development to occur in particular areas, and led to the evolution of mosquitoes resistant to insecticide. More pulp mills were built to process timber, fishing fleets expanded beyond their ability to maintain a sustainable yield of fish, more land areas were converted to cattle ranches and increased numbers of people are susceptible to malaria. At the same time, resource management agencies moved away from social and economic objectives and became narrowly focused on increasing such technical and operational efficiency as improved fire detection and control, improved navigation and more efficient delivery systems for insecticides (Holling 1986).

There are also examples of integrated approaches: some indigenous resource management systems, such as that of the Kayapo Indians, for example, appear to manage forests in a way that increases biodiversity and attracts game. A study by Anderson *et al.* (1991) illustrates the tight linkages between people and tropical forest resources, and suggests that these links may be the best long-term guarantee of resource conservation. Management of intact natural forests, a practice that is already widespread among rural populations in the tropics, has been neglected as an option because the benefits have been under-valued, and because the people who most depend on them are economically marginal and invisible to policy-makers. Secondary forests were found to provide several advantages for management in that they are extensive and accessible, are nature's response to human disturbance, are easily managed, are less complex and more resilient than primary forests and are exploited by rural populations for market and subsistence products. They are also integral components of land-use practices; for example, fallows are part of shifting cultivation. They support agroforestry systems that involve underplanting of crops or pasture grasses; they promote nutrient recycling and sustainability where people are already settled; and they reduce land-use pressure on primary forests.

Forest palms, for example, are important in market and in subsistence economies, occur on marginal sites unsuited to agriculture, may play a role in site restoration by recovering deep soil nutrients, provide food for game and domesticated animals and fruits that nourish aquatic communities. In the Brazilian Amazon alone, 1.5 million people depend on the extraction of latex, fibre, and fruits for a living, and generate revenues of $100 million a year, but they are vulnerable to more intrusive land uses. The babassu palm, in particular, flourishes on sites subject to human-induced disturbance and is the source of raw materials for an important cottage industry – the extraction of oil-rich kernels from hard, multilayered fruits for sale to landowners and merchants. This is mostly practiced by women and children and provides an important source of cash between crop harvests. Husks are used for charcoal – an important source of cooking fuel, leaves for basketry, thatch and fencing and stems are the source of palm hearts. The babassu palm also provides raw materials to the vegetable oil and feedcake industry. Kernels are the source of oils used in soaps and cosmetics and are the basis for the largest vegetable oil industry based entirely on a wild plant. The problem is that those most dependent on the babassu palm also have the least control of the forest, and their access to the resource is becoming increasingly restricted by more powerful competing interests (Anderson *et al.* 1991). Anderson *et al.* demonstrate that these resources provide an extensive subsidy to the local economy, and conclude that they should be perceived as a foundation for rather than as an obstacle to development.

The foundation for sustainable and integrated approaches to natural resource management is a system of maintaining natural resource accounts, as discussed in the next section. The section concludes with a discussion of integrated approaches to resource management through collective action. Following the last chapter is an Appendix with case studies that attempt to quantify the distribution of costs and benefits that result from different resource management options, to examine perverse incentives that result from some economic subsidies, and to discuss the less obvious costs and benefits in agriculture, and in the environmental restoration of urban squatter settlement.

Natural Resource Accounting

Changes in environmental conditions cannot be measured and quantified as precisely in economic terms as changes in material conditions because ecosystem values (as well as many human subsistence activities) are not usually accounted for. A standing forest, for example, provides real economic services by conserving soil, cleaning air and water, supplying fuelwood and non-timber products that are outside the market, providing habitat for wildlife and supporting recreational activities. But as GNP is currently calculated, only the value of harvested commercial timber is incorporated in the total. On the other hand, the billions of dollars that Exxon spent on the Valdez clean-up actually improved apparent economic performance because cleaning up oil spills creates jobs and consumes resources, all of which add to GNP. Of course, these expenses would not have been necessary if the oil had not been spilled, so they should not be considered as 'benefits'. But GNP adds up all market-oriented production without differentiating between costs and benefits, and is therefore not a very good measure of economic performance or health. Another problem with GNP is that the economic sectors contributing most to the GNP are also the most environmentally damaging; for example, automobiles contribute more to the GNP than do mass transit vehicles.

One reason that natural resources are not normally accounted for is because the costs of environmental degradation and resource depletion are not borne by the economic actors who cause them (Parikh *et al.* 1991). Because they often rely primarily and directly on natural resources, the poor bear these costs disproprtionately. Another reason is that, for damages that are irreversible such as the loss of biodiversity, economic valuation only provides a partial value. For example, a monetary cost-benefit analysis can be used to indicate monetary losses resulting from the loss of commercially harvested species, and willingness-to-pay may be used to determine aesthetic values. These methods are unable, however, to evaluate the role of species in the ecosystem, the overall extent to which ecosystems subsidize the human economy, and their value to future generations. A Natural Resource Accounting (NRA) system that includes non-market resources can, however, be used to value the assets of the poor, as well as to indicate the real income of a nation, how much is being borrowed from nature and from the future, and how much some members of society gain at the cost of others. Specifically, it could indicate current consumption, the extent to which resources must be imported to meet local demand, and where they are imported from. For example, one study that audited resource consumption in the Netherlands found that, in addition to the 3.4 million hectares that the Netherlands occupies, of which 2.9 million hectares are devoted to agriculture, an additional 5.3 million hectares are needed outside the country to meet the demands for domestic consumption and for the export industry – a situation that has led to the conversion of natural habitats in several developing countries (WRI, UNEP both 1992).

Methods proposed for adjusting the national accounts to reflect the depreciation of natural capital fall into two categories: summary NRA (Natural Resource Accounts) and Management-Oriented NRA (Lange and Duchin 1993). The summary NRA is calculated by subtracting the estimated monetary value of the net depletion of natural resources from national gross and net income to produce an Environmentally Adjusted Domestic Product (EDP). The depletion value can be measured, for example by the change over the accounting period in sales, minus production costs. This approach limits itself to marketed resources (e.g., timber and petroleum) or those that contribute directly to market production (e.g., gróundwater) for which economic values can be estimated based on market values. Resources that do not contribute directly to market production, such as the non-marketed services of rivers and forests, are not addressed by this method because it is difficult to assign them monetary values (Perrings and Opschoor 1994).

A Management-Oriented NRA consists of a more comprehensive set of measurements designed to provide data that can be used in input-output models for analysis of the economic and environmental implications of alternative policies and scenarios for sustainable development. This is done by constructing satellite accounts that record the stock and flow of material resources in physical units. These accounts include extraction, uses in production and consumption and discharge of waste materials for each economic sector, including households.

Summary Natural Resource Accounts

Examples of summary NRA are the World Resources Institute studies of Costa Rica and Indonesia. The Costa Rica study calculated that forests, fisheries, agriculture and mines contributed 17% of the national income, 28% of employment and 55% of export earnings. In the System of National Accounts (SNA), these revenues are treated as factor income rather than as capital consumption. The practice of converting forest land to cattle pasture, which ruins the soil and is not economically viable, was treated as capital investment even though banks are losing $382 million annually in uncollectable loans to the cattle industry. The study (Repetto 1991) concluded that this trend would exhaust Costa Rica's commercial forests within five years, and threaten the country's long-term prosperity. Forest products would also have to be imported.

Some critics of this method point out that it does not consider the issue of re-investment. For example, nations that rely heavily on non-renewable resources might appear to have a net income of zero while enjoying high levels of consumption. However, a nation reinvesting some proceeds in order to replace the soon-to-be depleted resource with a new asset of equal value may not actually be decreasing its wealth. They also contend that Repetto's approach does not adequately account for the creation of new wealth caused by the destruction of natural resource wealth. In other words, the destruction may not be sufficiently treated as an 'investment' in conventional income accounts (if the new wealth is in the public sector) (Peskin and Lutz 1990). According to this view, since the growth in GDP is used to evaluate a country's performance, and policies are shaped according to their contributions to the GDP, it is important that the GDP reflects the actual conditions of the economy.

Both the summary method, as well as the above criticism, appear to assume a high degree of substitutability between natural and produced capital – an assumption that is being increasingly questioned as we come to terms with the complexity of natural systems. For example, the cost of soil degradation is calculated as the cost of commercial fertilizer that is required to replace lost nutrients, an approach that ignores other soil qualities such as soil structure (Lange and Duchin 1993). Barbier (1990) expresses this view thus:

'...more recent theories now stress the limits to "substitution" between many forms of natural and man-made capital, even for developing countries interested in "drawing down" their natural capital stock in favor of investing in other forms of capital. From an ecological standpoint, a major factor is the failure to consider the economic consequences of the loss in "resilience", "the ability of ecosystems to cope with random shocks and prolonged stress" that results from natural capital depletion.'

The results of a summary NRA may also vary widely depending on how values are established for non-marketed resources and for environmental degradation. This gives rise to interpretation problems because these imputed costs are hypothetical and are not reflected in market prices. Methods of valuation proposed for use with the NRA include avoidance cost, repair cost and contingent valuation. A key problem with all of these valuation techniques is that they 'rely on prices established in well-functioning "surrogate" markets which often do not exist in developing countries, e.g., labour and capital markets' (Lange and Duchin 1993). Other problems associated with using these valuation techniques in NRA are illustrated by the following example:

'...discharge into a river of a toxic substance which could have been avoided by the use of low cost controls. Even though the discharge was not avoided, the avoidance cost method would value the environmental degradation at this low cost. The actual damage in this example can be extensive if fish and wildlife are killed and the water is rendered unfit for agriculture or other human use. Thus, the cost of clean-up, or the repair cost, is very high. If there is irreversible damage, the cost of restoring the river may be infinite. The willingness-to-pay approach may produce values that are either very high or very low, depending upon the incomes of the population and how well-informed they are. Similarly, willingness-to-accept could produce a wide range of values' (Lange and Duchin 1993).

The EDP is therefore not based on a consistent value system and, like the GNP, excludes human capital and non-market economic activities in the informal sector; it also provides little guidance on how sustainable development might be achieved (Lange and Duchin 1993; Opschoor 1992). Next to GNP or other consistent indicators for economic performance, social and environmental indicators (in their own dimensions) may be developed to provide a broad set of tools for monitoring change in the current and future welfare base (Opschoor and Reijnders 1991).

Management-Oriented Natural Resource Accounts

A management-oriented approach to NRA is reflected in the satellite System of Integrated Environmental and Economic Accounting (SEEA) proposed by the United Nations Statistical Office. This system, while following many principles outlined in the System of National Accounts (SNA), attempts also to account for changes in the quality of the environment and depletion of natural resources.

The current SNA recommended by the United Nations is more complete in terms of natural resource accounting NRA than are the accounting systems actually utilized by most nations. Most countries limit their national accounting to the basic economic indicators of GDP, GDP growth per capita and the rate of inflation. Under the SNA, balance sheets record increases and decreases in a country's assets – including tangible natural assets such as tree plantations, agricultural lands and subsoil minerals. These assets, however, must be privately owned and used in the commercial production of goods and services in order for economic values to be established.

The proposed SEEA would extend the concept of capital to include 'natural' in addition to 'man-made' capital, and would incorporate non-monetary data on the stocks and flows of natural resources into the accounting system. The goal of the proposed SEEA is to assess the environmental costs and benefits of economic activities by accounting for the use or depletion of natural resources in production and final demand as well as changes in environmental quality. This expansion means the SEEA will include costs incurred by the depletion and degradation of natural assets and may reflect the transfer of natural capital for economic use (Bartelmus, Lutz and Schweinfest 1992).

Lastly, the SEEA allows for the calculation of an Environmentally Adjusted Net Domestic Product (EDP), which takes into consideration the depletion of natural resources and changes in environmental quality (Bartelmus, Lutz and Schweinfest 1992). Degradation and depletion costs are deducted from the GDP to determine the EDP; damages incurred by natural causes or unrelated to production activities, however, are not utilized in this calculation.

Although the natural damage costs would not be included in calculating the

EDP, they would be considered in the calculation of an Environmentally Adjusted Net Income (ENI). This figure would be calculated by subtracting five items from the EDP: (1) government and household environmental protection expenditures; (2) the costs of environmental effects on health and other facets of human capital; (3) environmental costs of household and government consumption activities; (4) the costs of environmental damage caused by discarding capital goods; and (5) the costs of negative environmental effects in the country that are caused by another country. According to Munasinghe and Lutz, EDP would more accurately measure sustainable income because it would 'better capture environmental services, account for the depreciation of both man-made and natural capital, exclude relevant categories of defensive environmental expenditures, and/or estimate damages as a result of economic activities.'

The management-oriented approach to NRA is only effective if it is responsive to policy questions identified at the initial stages. It is also a more ambitious undertaking because it requires physical information on stocks and flows of natural resources, disaggregated by economic sector, including the consumption and non-market activities of households. It can then be used in the input-output modelling framework currently used for national accounts, to integrate economic and environmental sectors, to determine trade-offs among development strategies, and to determine the implications of alternative economic valuation methods. A uniform classification scheme can also integrate data gathered in different government agencies and political jurisdictions into a common analytical framework that can be used to identify inconsistencies and inter-relationships. Much of this information is currently gathered in an *ad hoc* manner because there are no standard methods for doing this (Lange and Duchin 1993).

The modelling process can then be used to examine the implications of particular policies, such as structural adjustment or removal of subsidies, and to identify the most vulnerable sectors and cumulative effects throughout the economy. A model might show, for example, how a particular cost increase such as for fuel would directly or indirectly affect particular sectors of the economy and the extent to which substitution by fuelwood and increased deforestation might be an option. It might also illustrate trade-offs between potentially higher export earnings and loss of subsistence crops leading to the impoverishment of rural populations and associated kinds of environmental degradation (Lange and Duchin 1993).

Because of the commitment of human and financial resources required to develop management-oriented NRA, a modular approach is suggested, one that allows for user feedback and modification to ensure it is responsive to the unique circumstances to which it is being applied, reflects change and meets the needs of policy-makers. Developing countries, for example, may place greater emphasis on informal sectors of the economy and on natural resources, while industrialized countries will be more concerned with pollution issues. However, as heavy and more polluting industries are becoming increasingly concentrated in developing countries, those countries will also need to become concerned with industrial pollution. Developed countries, on the other hand, need to account for the scale of resource consumption and the extent to which it preempts the development options of the poor.

A natural resource accounting system proposed for India, for example, identifies the main assets of interest as agricultural land, forests, water, air, biodiversity, and exhaustible resources. This is because India is a poor and populous country in which agriculture supplies 30% of GDP and engages 65% of the population, and in which most people spend the bulk of their income on food. Forests sustain a large tribal population, are a major source of fuel, and are important for preserving soil. In addition, virgin forests are a source of biodiversity that has been valued and preserved by Indian cultural traditions that respect other forms of life. The value of biodiversity as a resource is also reflected in ethnic knowledge of herbal medicines that are important to those who either cannot afford modern medicines, or who find traditional products more effective. This knowledge also includes biological indicators for weather changes, signals for extreme events, water purifying techniques and preservatives. Herbal medicines and cosmetics also provide export earnings. Water supply is crucial for agriculture, and water quality is a high priority because of the prevalence of water-borne diseases, and the reliance on fish for protein in several parts of the country. Poor air quality is a problem in metropolitan areas, and in the kitchens of those who depend on biomass fuels, and who have a high incidence of respiratory diseases and eye infections.

This proposed system emphasizes the importance of separating large- and small-scale production because the small-scale sector employs a substantial number of people and generates a large portion of the GNP. Consumption should distinguish the manner of consumption (e.g., public transport vs. private cars) and types of fuel that have different environmental consequences. Population is obviously important in determining the scale of consumption, for comparison with other countries and for projecting trends.

Integrated Approaches to Natural Resource Management

Integrated approaches to natural resource management are a prerequisite for sustainable development because agriculture, forestry and fisheries as well as being non-renewable resources feed people, provide raw materials that are the basis for all consumption, and are the most affected by conflicting demands for development and environmental protection. According to FAO (1993), 'achieving sustainability in these areas will be the foundation for a lasting balance between environmental, social, and economic goals'. In order to do this, it is important to analyse policies that have been adopted to achieve other social goals in order to determine whether they have secondary effects that detract from sustainability; and to focus on policies that contribute to sustainability (FAO 1993). As is discussed throughout this report, many current policies actively discriminate against these sectors. Resource management needs to go beyond the use of technology packages. According to FAO (1993), while these may seem straightforward and easy to apply, a large gap remains between crop potentials and the average farmer's yields because of 'high prices, and the unavailability of recommended inputs; weak market demand for outputs; lack of effective ways of disseminating technology, particularly information-based technology; unfavourable land tenure systems; and lack of credit and marketing facilities'. Inputs could be reduced by reducing the need for them, through diversified cropping systems that limit pests, biological pest control measures, integrated plant nutrient systems, and by generally taking advantage of biological processes such as the use of nitrogen-fixing plants, rotating crops, using trees as 'nutrient pumps' and recycling wastes – techniques already used by farmers with little or no access to external inputs.

These techniques require increased understanding of the ecosystem, cooperation among farmers and researchers, and sharing of information. For example, integrated pest management (IPM) is based on the ecology of plant pest and livestock interactions, which can be modified through the diversification of cropping patterns and systems to create more complex ecological interactions and cycles so that beneficial insects and microorganisms can thrive and naturally suppress damaging pests, and is combined with the selective use of pesticides. Integrated Plant Nutrition (IPN) can be used to reduce the need for fertilizers, because it is based on accounts of nutrient flows into and out of the system to determine where and why imbalances occur. Fertilizers are then used to correct imbalances rather than being indiscriminately applied. FAO suggests that these accounts could be incorporated into regional and national nutrient accounts, which could then be used to assess the availability and cost of alternative sources of plant nutrients. These might include the use of composting technology to produce soil additives from unusual sources of biomass, such as wastes generated by aquaculture or the local use of biomass for energy (FAO 1993). Conservation of genetic resources could be made economically feasible through the development and use of indigenous varieties and finding ways to compensate communities for the use of their genetic resources elsewhere. One important means of protecting agricultural biological diversity is to involve local inhabitants in the management of protected habitats.

In order to implement these kinds of strategies, stronger institutions are required for resource management. Human cultures may be viewed as systems of resource management, and as has been discussed throughout this report, environmental degradation is the consequence of a breakdown in human institutions that determine the nature of resource management, or the loss of what we may call 'cultural capital'. The concept of cultural capital includes the diversity of ways that societies relate to their environment, their concept of nature, their values and their understanding of the environment, including traditional ecological knowledge. Resource management institutions have also been defined as 'the conventions that societies establish to define their members' relationships to resources, translate interests in resources into claims, and claims into property rights' (Gibbs and Bromley 1989). In other words, our world view, values, knowledge, and institutions shape the way in which we treat the environment.

Culture also implies commonality, and provides the basis for collective action. It has been observed that 'given a resource management problem, a group of people often organize themselves to deal with it in a manner similar to the formation of a "bucket brigade" to put out a fire in a rural neighborhood'. These self-organizing capabilities observed in social systems are analogous to those in ecosystems and may be harnessed to increase efficiency in resource use. (The implications of losing these capabilities have been described as a 'new species of trouble' (Erikson 1994) and are extensively discussed in the section on the impacts of environmental stress and resource exploitation on the poor).

What most success stories appear to have in common is a primary focus on collective institutional arrangements for cooperation and a shared sense of responsibility. There have been some noteworthy innovative approaches. A group of 26 private companies in Mexico City pooled their resources by contributing equity, in proportion to their water needs, to rehabilitate a municipal wastewater treatment plant. As a result they were able to obtain treated water for the shareholder companies at 75% of the cost charged by the government, and provided a substantial amount of treated water to the government as payment for the concession to operate the plant. In a Karachi squatter settlement, with the help of a community organizer, the members of the community developed their own organization to provide sanitation services in innovative ways at an affordable cost (less than $100 per household). In a French river basin, a water parliament was formed of representatives of government and non-government agencies and interested parties in order to manage externalities, generated by municipalities, by establishing charges for water extraction and for pollution depending on the needs of the river basin. The revenues are then used for water supply and wastewater treatment facilities. An innovative lower-cost sewer system in Brazil worked well because of community involvement in maintaining feeder sewers from individual homes, which were all interconnected, while the utility remained responsible only for trunk mains (Briscoe 1993).

Water is a major source of conflict because it exists in limited supply, because upstream users may deprive those downstream, and because it usually flows across political boundaries. This aspect of water may also make it a key to the development of more equitable and sustainable institutional arrangements for resource management through the establishment of international river basin authorities. As in the French river basin, these authorities should include representatives of all interested parties and would monitor externalities and account for natural resource depreciation as the basis for an adaptive management strategy and would intimately involve those who are most affected in the management of resources. Such a strategy could also become the basis for local as well as global conflict resolution by facilitating the development of relationships based on trust and cooperation.

As discussed throughout this report, management of resources for narrowly focused objectives normally has unintended ecological and economic consequences that may impoverish disadvantaged social groups, or disproportionately affect those who are already poor, in addition to degrading the environment. Devising a strategy for ecologically sustainable development might begin by identifying available resources, and considering how existing levels might be used more efficiently, rather than how more might be obtained (Clarke 1993). Improved management and allocation can then be used to enforce limitations. Water resources, for example, have generally been managed by command and control because there are no mechanisms to signal the effects of one use of water on other potential users. Irrigation is heavily subsidized, with users paying on average only 10% or less of the operating cost. Modest reallocations could meet most urban demands, where higher prices for water delivery could be used to finance improved irrigation efficiency. Use of effluent charges to internalize at least some of the costs of disposal also reduced water demand up to 62% in three industrial plants in São Paulo. Developers could also be required to invest in public sewer systems as part of the cost of building houses (Briscoe 1993).

One way to reconcile conflicting objectives is to examine alternative development strategies using integrated regional ecological and economic models. This is an exercise that can provide feedback on environmental conditions relative to management objectives; identify ecological and social non-market economic subsidies; illustrate the distribution of environmental costs and benefits that would result from different types of resource use; and actual or potential land use and value conflicts; and any other important elements that need to be considered in a landscape model. This type of model could then be the basis for the adaptive management of resources and for explicitly identifying any trade-offs being made between meeting short-term and long-term needs, and for political decisions.

One good starting point for meaningful public participation in the process of establishing community and regional goals for conservation and in ecologically sustainable development, might be to develop maps, based on indigenous and local knowledge, that reflect traditional and/or actual land uses. Where such maps were produced, in Honduras and in Panama, by cartographers in collaboration with indigenous surveyors, it was found that 'the remaining forest, savanna and wetland almost perfectly overlap with indigenous territories', and the resulting maps were more accurate in their proportions than existing government maps. The project also made the indigenous inhabitants more visible to policy-makers, and provided documentation to help establish previously unrecognized land rights. At a subsequent forum, indigenous groups had the opportunity to present their perspective on land use, their understanding of the local ecosystem, and threats to their way of life to an audience that included government officials, local and international NGOs, and other indigenous groups. 'By centering the forums around the scientific maps and technical evaluations, the Indians had built a graphic and credible base from which to launch political campaigns on several issues, including legalizing communal homelands, stemming the incursions of colonization by settlers, and development by multinational companies, and resolving the relationship between Indian homelands and national protected areas.'

CONCLUSIONS AND RECOMMENDA'

Development and Sustainability

Development is sustainable if the management of resources, the direction of investments, the orientation of technological innovation and institutional change are harmonized and enhance both current and future potential to meet human needs and aspirations (WCED 1987). This implies an ongoing pursuit of the eradication of poverty and environmental degradation. As these often have related root causes, fighting one of these two will frequently imply gains with respect to the other.

Sustainable development requires that (1) the scale of development be sustainable in biophysical terms, (2) a proper balance between present and future demands on resources be made, and (3) inequity of all kinds (that results in creating either unsustainable scales and/or the unduly high levels of present consumption at the cost of the future and/or impoverishes one group at the cost of the other) be kept within limits.

This is indeed a challenging task and will require the harnessing of different kinds of policy instruments. Additionally, it will also be necessary to build sustainability requirements into the working of major institutions.

The scale issue is probably the most contentious. Economics solves it by concentrating on scarce resources and defining the scale of production as that which can be achieved, given these constraints, most of the time within the framework of the market. It has in the past treated natural resources and environmental quality as being essentially unlimited. Once it is recognized that they are not, economic decision-making will have to adjust accordingly. At times, this may require the use of institutions other than the market and of policy instruments other than the choice of appropriate technology. Recent studies have shown that it is unlikely that the earth can sustainably support the continued economic growth that would be necessary for all countries to have the life-style and level of resource consumption taking place primarily in developed countries but also in some enclaves within some developing countries as well. This raises a number of questions revolving around the nature of the alternatives and their viability in economic, social and political terms.

In considering the next crucial dimension of sustainability it is important so see that resources are time and space specific. Each ecosystem that has survived has done so because it operates within a set of parameters that are conducive to its requirements. Communities and institutions developed rules for use of resources that have enabled inter-temporal sustainability to be maintained. This could have been either by keeping the scales of current consumption within limits, or by ensuring the existence of alternative institutions or even by limiting populations to sustainable levels. The challenge before the international community now is to recognize the space and ecosystem specific role played by community-oriented structures in the preservation of resources and to reward them appropriately, notwithstanding the global movement towards uniformity of institutional structures. For example, property rights designations at the international level need to take account of community-based property rights as well.

A key criterion for sustainable development is that it should not ultimately impoverish one group as it enriches another. A pattern marked by growing inequity may be sustainable in purely biophysical terms, but its social sustainability requires the perpetual political control of low-income groups or countries (Gallopin *et al.* 1989). Failure to meet the needs of the least advantaged also perpetuates an economic system that achieves growth at the expense of human and environmental impoverishment. Internalizing these costs will require a restructuring of the economy in order to meet human needs by investing in human and natural capital.

Development policies may be designed to target individual producers or consumers (e.g., through special credit programmes, or food subsidies) or whole communities (e.g., literacy programmes, preventive health care). They may be designed to integrate rural and urban areas through investments in infrastructure (e.g., water supply, communications, roads), or may be designed to remove institutional barriers that block access to resources by the poor (e.g., land reform). They may also address macro-economic conditions and indirectly have substantial micro-economic, social and environmental repercussions, as is the case with structural adjustment policies. Policies aiming at sustainable development should take into account considerations related to: (1) the scale of resource consumption, (2) equitable distribution of and access to resources, and (3) allocative efficiency.

Two directions of policy have been suggested so far: the use of existing institutions and the range of policy instruments that they offer to limit scales of development where they exceed the levels that are sustainable and the creation of new institutions that recognize the special nature of the relationship between communities and resources.

In striving for sustainability, the entire range of institutions should be considered, including the market. Economic reforms and development policies based on an economic approach have mostly been concerned with allocative efficiency to be achieved through marginal adjustments using market mechanisms. These kinds of measures have little effect on poverty and sustainability, unless they are accompanied by structural changes to address problems related to the scale of consumption and equitable distribution. Markets may not generate the signals of environmental stress in time because environmental services are for the most part external to the market, and the problem may have become irreversible by the time such signals are generated. In addition, markets can only address problems of allocative efficiency – problems of sustainable scale and equitable distribution must be decided first and through democratic social dialogue. Economics in the past concerned itself primarily with the scarcity of labour and manufactured capital, treating natural resources and environmental quality as essentially unlimited. Now that these have become recognized as primary limiting factors, it is necessary to establish limits to the scale of the economy in the political arena and internalize these limits as social values by developing new, more adaptive institutions that can provide social resilience in the face of ecological variability. Market mechanisms can then be used for allocative purposes within these socially defined limits and goals. Moreover, market prices can often be corrected for unaccounted environmental and resource costs (see below); wherever such corrections can be made governments should consider using these as a policy instrument.

Sustainable development implies a policy of 'merging environment and economics in decision making' (WCED 1987). This means: (1) bringing environmental and resource costs to bear on prices, and (2) establishing proper accounting systems at the macro-level.

Especially in developing countries, inefficient use or even exhaustion of natural resources may occur, due – *inter alia* – to missing or malfunctioning markets. Policies must be put in place to address this, and interventions directed at market failures are a necessary component. But in addition, safe standards and zoning in order to protect minimum qualities and quantities of the environmental infrastructure might be necessary.

Turning to accounting aspects, several points are worth considering. Welfare and income run parallel only if: (1) income is corrected for depreciation in all stocks of resources, and (2) income fully reflects the externalities of production and consumption processes. From the point of view of sustainable development, these two conditions are far from being fulfilled. Net National Income structurally overestimates sustainable income; policies for which GNP is used as a welfare indicator may be incompatible with, or unconducive towards, sustainable development. These shortcomings of GNP as a welfare indicator should be taken into account by national governments but also by multilateral institutions when drawing up development and intervention programmes. Indicators other than economic ones (social and environmental) should be used to get an impression of the environmental depreciations and externalities that are involved in intervention programmes.

Policy Recommendations

Achievement of sustainability is a long-term process that will require investment in human and natural capital as well as significant political will. Investments in human capital, however, contribute to the development of political capital because they enable poor people to participate in the political decisions necessary for the protection of natural capital. There are immediate actions that can be taken to begin to move in the right direction. These actions range from policies at the level of individuals and communities to those at national and global level. An integrated, multi-scale approach is necessary in order to reap the benefits of small-scale adaptive management while still recognizing and incorporating large scale goals and constraints.

Policies could be divided into those that have a direct impact on resource use and those that aim at giving a new structure to instruments of institutions and/or evolving new instruments or institutions. A third set of policies relates to human or political capital creation and the building up of methodologies, such as national income accounting, which ensure that the significance of natural capital is built into the statistical systems of different countries in the same fashion as other components of national income accounting.

1. Investment in Natural Capital

To the extent that natural capital is becoming a main limiting factor, it needs to be the focus of investments in sustainable development. Investment in natural capital implies maximizing its productivity in the short run, and increasing its supply in the long run.

Tax Consumption, Throughput and the Associated Depletion and Pollution One instrument for investing in natural capital would be simply to shift our tax base away from labour and income on to throughput. The present system for raising revenue is highly distortionary in that, by taxing labour and income in the face of high unemployment in nearly all countries, we are discouraging exactly what we want more of. The present signal to firms is to shed labour, and substitute more capital and resource throughput, to the extent feasible. It would be better to economize on throughput because of the high external costs of its associated depletion and pollution, and at the same time to use more labour because of the high social benefits associated with reducing unemployment. The income tax structure should be maintained so as to keep progressivity in the overall tax structure by taxing very high incomes and subsidizing very low incomes. But the bulk of public revenue would be raised from taxes on throughput, either at the depletion or pollution end. This shift should be a key part of structural adjustment, but should be pioneered in the North. Since multilateral institutions do not have leverage over the North, this kind of measure may require strong grassroots political pressure.

Ensure Internationalization of Environmental Externalities in Prices As many as possible of the environmental externalities need to be internalized by way of prices. The use of scarce resources, such as water and forests, by agriculture or industry, needs to be given a certain cost which is in line with their resource cost. Similarly, the creation of atmospheric pollution by industry should be treated as the use of a scarce resource for which a price has to be paid. Structural adjustment programmes need to recognize this adjustment as an integral part of their policy of 'setting prices right'.

Commodity prices should fully internalize the human and environmental costs of their production. This is an important first step towards global sustainability because they provide the raw materials upon which all consumption is based, and because agriculture is central to the connection between the ecosystem and the human economy. As discussed in this report, smallholder agriculture is often more efficient in terms of the ratio of energy inputs to product yield, helps to preserve biodiversity, and can provide a stable base of employment. Smallholder agriculture also provides a supportive base for rural communities because it has a strong economic multiplier effect. This in turn contributes to the development of stronger institutions for the conservation of natural resources.

Support Ecologically Appropriate Technologies Ecological engineering is an important area for sustainable development because it requires low capital investment and inputs of fossil fuels, because it relies primarily on the self-organizing properties of ecosystems, and on human inputs. It may also take advantage of abandoned resources and be used for ecological restoration. It is already extensively used in China in the areas of agriculture, wastewater treatment, management of fish cultures and the design of human communities so as to take advantage of ecological functions. This kind of technology pays particular attention to the utilization of wastes and recycling (Mitsch 1991).

As a part of fiscal policy, industry recycling waste and/or conserving the use of natural resources could be given concessional tax treatment.

Support Sustainable Structural Adjustment Structural adjustment programmes, such as those carried out by the World Bank, should support a transition to ecologically sustainable economic development, based on long-term social and environmental objectives determined through a democratic process. To further that process, the World Bank might enhance the development of natural resource accounting systems that, as discussed below, could provide information to facilitate public participation in the valuation of natural resources and provide the basis for internalizing non-market costs. Also, structural adjustment programmes could support the development of social institutions for the enforcement of environmental protection laws, and the protection of the land rights of poor and indigenous communities.

The World Bank aims at 'weak sustainability', but in practice traditional ideas on economic growth and development still play an important role. Sustainable development will benefit from adjustment policies that pursue the removal of price distortions through the elimination of market and government failures. To safeguard future development potentials, long-term maintenance of absolute minimum environmental qualities and resources should be targeted. Better still would be to assure safe minimum standards, though this might as yet be unfeasible for many developing countries. Financial and technical support of industrialized countries might turn out to be indispensable in going beyond bare minimum levels of environmental protection in the poorer developing countries. Institutional changes such as introduction of property rights are necessary to correct for market and government failures that hamper the realization and maintenance of sustainability. Macro-economic adjustments should trigger and stimulate sustainable development and certainly should not further unsustainability. Implementation of complementary environmental projects might provide a short-term solution to situations of incidental environmental degradation caused by intervention programmes.

In the long run, it may be potentially more in line with sustainability to replace the strategy of fostering unrestricted trade liberalization and exported growth with one that aims at strengthening economies by developing domestic and regional markets.

Adapt Trade Policies Exchange under unfair conditions may result in net transfers of wealth to the North. Ensuring that trade and environment are mutually supportive entails the internalization of environmental externalities and future resource scarcities.

Problems related to trade versus environment may arise as conflicts due to the absence of a multinational regulator, conflicts over instruments and conflicts over the use of trade measures for environmental purposes. These issues should be addressed in the new World Trade Organization; a precautionary approach to irreversible degradation, the principle that polluters and users pay for claims on the environment, and appropriate instruments or appropriately harmonized approaches of products and PPMs, are elements of long-term sustainable solutions to these problems.

Improve Natural Resource Accounting The orientation in most accounting systems is on traditional economic indicators such as GNP. These indicators do not give adequate information on sustainable income, thus threatening future sustainable development. A solution to this might be the use of social and environmental indicators in addition to the economic indicators. A consistent system of accounting for natural resource depreciation is necessary in order to identify environmental costs and benefits and their distribution. This is also important for correcting inequities because poor people rely primarily on natural resources that are not valued in the market and pay a disproportionate share of the costs of environmental degradation. Natural resource accounting systems can also provide the basis for scientific and political dialogue to determine the proper scale of economic activities relative to the earth's carrying capacity, to establish long-term social and environmental objectives, and for fair trade. Maps of land capabilities, current land uses and degradation, can be used to assess options for sustainable development, and to integrate land management into economic and social policy, e.g., to integrate reforestation and other development assistance into local agricultural and economic settings. These methods should be used in a participatory, consensus-building framework in order to achieve maximum benefits.

2. Policies Aiming at Coordination between International, National and Local-level Institutions

The processes of globalization and the spread of information technology have made the concept of the global village a reality. Simultaneously, micro-level studies have revealed that sustainable use of local resources is best achieved through management at local levels. In the presence of market and government failures, it is recognized that new cooperative institutions need to be strengthened. Areas to be allocated to these need to be spelt out, possibly with national governments acting as mediating agencies. One general rule could be that whenever natural resources that enter into the livelihoods of people are involved, local-level management should be given preference.

The Micro Level A key objective of development should be to enable disadvantaged households to widen their decision-making horizon and extend their time-frame. This implies the need to find incentives for short-term behaviour that are consistent with long-term goals of resource management. Improving access to resources is another important strategy, but in order for improved access to be sustainable, it must be accompanied by the establishment of accountable and participatory institutions and better defined rights to resources.

One reason for the failure of many natural resource management initiatives is the insistence on a standardized approach. Appropriate variability in design or organization, and options for sustainable resource use, cannot be conceptualized without an understanding of the variability of ecological endowments. Any framework which ignores the multi-market, multi-enterprise and multi-institutional dimensions of household portfolios provides only a partial understanding of people's survival logic. In developing policy scenarios, especially at the national level, this should be taken into account.

The need for community participation in development projects has been increasingly recognized by organizations involved in development assistance. National governments are recommended to consider decentralized approaches to their social and development programmes. Such decentralization would be likely to increase the efficiency of government development spending, because projects should be more selectively suited to local needs, local employment should increase and, since the community will in a sense be spending its 'own' money and residents will feel more included in the process, there will be an added incentive to lower cost and increase performance.

Recognition and Enforcement of Property Rights Recognition of traditional land rights and enforcement of those rights can provide the assurances needed by the poor to lengthen their time-horizons and thus broaden their options for resource management. This recognition needs to include traditional land tenure arrangements, such as common property regimes, which are important for the sustainable use of resources under conditions of high ecological variability.

Common property regimes, as opposed to open access, can also provide an institutional framework for internalizing externalities by recognizing poor people as stakeholders in the management of natural resources. As discussed in this report, common ownership of the capacity of the earth to absorb waste, previously treated as a 'free good', would greatly increase the cost of disposal and act as a powerful incentive to reduce consumption. A common property framework can also facilitate the collective action that is needed for integrated approaches to sustainable development, through the pooling of knowledge and resources.

Land Reform Land reform could significantly relieve pressure on marginal and ecologically fragile lands because, in many developing countries, distribution is highly skewed, with most agricultural land being concentrated in a small percentage of holdings. For example, in Paraguay, a recent survey found that 1% of all farms had more than 1,000 hectares and accounted for 78% of the land, while 37% of the farms had less than 5 hectares and accounted for less than 1% of the land. Land reform may, however, be the most politically difficult to achieve among all the recommendations listed because land distribution generally reflects the power structure within a country, and land distribution programmes usually meet with strong political resistance. When land reform efforts have been carried out, it has often been to the benefit of medium-size farmers within the modern agricultural sector rather than the poorest groups (FAO 1993). In some cases, such as Indonesia and Thailand, instead of redistributing land, governments have distributed previously uncultivated and uncleared forest areas to alleviate poverty while simultaneously protecting the *status quo* of elites (Reed 1992). Perhaps it is more practical to approach land reform indirectly, as a desired outcome of other kinds of efforts that contribute to the restructuring of power relations.

Strengthening of International Authority The globalization of the economy through free trade weakens national boundaries and the power of national and subnational communities, while strengthening the relative power of transnational corporations (TNCs). 'Global competitiveness' may simply mean a standards-lowering competition to reduce wages, externalize environmental and social costs, and export natural capital at low prices while calling it income. In 1980, of the 100 biggest economic entities, half were countries and half were TNCs. Transnational corporations easily escape the law of one country by taking refuge in another. Although their actions may have global effects, they may be effectively out of reach (Gallopin *et al.* 1989). TNCs have little vested interest in regional sustainability because, when one region becomes over-exploited, they may simply move elsewhere. TNCs should at a minimum be held accountable to the laws of host countries and, where necessary because of weak environmental laws, to stricter standards of their home countries (WRI; UNEP both 1992).

International institutions need to be strengthened for purposes of understanding and addressing global-scale problems and to keep transnational corporations accountable to the common good. Ironically, one of the ways to strengthen international institutions is to strengthen national authority, because international agreements presuppose the ability of national governments to carry out policies in their support. If nations have no control over their borders they are in a poor position to enforce national laws, including those necessary to secure compliance with international treaties.

One may discern three tiers of development institutions: international developmental organizations, national governments and grassroots organizations. The overall challenge is to evolve structures for development that are able to coordinate effectively these three tiers. Within this setting, the challenge for development organizations is to see themselves as participants in governmental development efforts as well as to find ways to liaise with and reinforce grassroots efforts, and thus to be a link between local and global systems. International organizations can act as a catalyst for social action by providing a base of common knowledge and by helping to strengthen social organization to increase the capacity of the poor for collective action to control access to their resources.

Role of International NGOs Poverty levels have gone beyond being a massive global outrage to being perhaps a global-scale disaster requiring massive international cooperation in relief efforts, as well as in removing the obstacles to sustainable development. Integrated approaches are needed to alleviate poverty and protect the environment by tapping and protecting the productivity of both human and natural capital. Certain societies, traumatized by political, economic and ecological shocks, may need catalysers to regain their organizational and creative capabilities (Ben Abdallah and Engelhard 1993). NGOs can play an important role by enhancing communications between groups.

3. *Investment in Human Capital through Improvements in Nutrition, Education and Health*

At the individual level, investment in human capital can begin to reverse the downward spiral of human and environmental impoverishment. Improvements in nutrition, health and education can lengthen the time-horizons of the poor and strengthen their ability to combat the environmental degradation of which they are victims, and contribute to voluntary diminution of population growth. Although addressing illness, malnutrition, poor growth, and illiteracy does not directly address the causes of poverty, such as debt burdens and inequitable economic relationships, it is crucial because these problems undermine the long-term development process.

Historically, improvement of water and sanitation services were a major factor in increasing life expectancy and in improving the quality of life in the developed countries, and can have big payoffs for sustainable development. For example, over a 10 year period, death rates from typhoid fever declined more than 80% in cities that treated their water in the Ohio River valley. It is estimated that current rates of child mortality from diarrhoea could be reduced by 2 million a year. Poor water quality reduced the marketability of fruits and vegetable in export markets in Chile, and cholera epidemics caused tourism revenue in Peru to drop by more than three times the amount that had been invested in water and sanitation in the 1980s (Briscoe 1993). Reducing the amount of time needed to obtain water supplies – often 15% of a woman's time – would also vastly improve the lives of women.

According to UNICEF, the ideal point of intervention in the downward spiral of poverty is at the prenatal stage and in the early years of life. Breastmilk, which can provide a standard of nutrition during the years of most rapid physical and mental growth, during which humans are the most vulnerable, is not affected by the socio-economic level of the family into which a child is born. They advocate that children be placed at the centre of development thinking because of the relationship between the physical and mental needs of children and the social and economic development of their societies.

Improving the quality of the lives of women can trigger a multiplier effect because of their multiple roles in raising children, in education and as managers of natural resources in providing for their families. Priorities would include access to health care, education, land and credit. Improvements in the human capital of the poor majority, notably in health and education, historically have been associated with declining fertility for a number of reasons: women gain greater access to employment opportunities outside the home; lower infant and child mortality mean fewer births are needed to attain a given probability of survival to adulthood; the importance of children's labour in family income diminishes; access to birth control and supporting health services improves; and so on (Cassen 1976; Repetto 1979; Caldwell 1982). Insofar as population growth exacerbates environmental degradation – and there are undoubtedly settings where, all else being equal, it does so – this demographic transition constitutes a further link between human capital and natural capital (Segura and Boyce 1994).

With better nutrition, health and education, the poor become better able to resist the economic and political pressures of the rich; better able to analyse the causes and consequences of environmental degradation; and better able to score victories in the political arenas where conflicts are ultimately resolved. The complementarity between human capital and natural capital is here mediated by what can be termed the 'political capital' of the poor (Segura and Boyce 1994).

The possible effects on birth rates of this shift in the balance of power merits comment. Greater power for the poor – especially for women – increases the political effectiveness of their demand for access to birth control and reproductive health services. By the same token, however, it strengthens their capacity to resist unwanted birth control measures pushed upon them by governments in the name of population control. For example, improvements in living standards in Bangladesh might reduce the number of women who accept sterilization in return for 'incentive' payments in the form of cash and clothing (Hartmann 1987). Evidence from the field suggests that there exists a demand for birth control measures and smaller families. Rural women, in particular when faced with resource-scarce situations, seem to understand the need for smaller families. Also, user-friendly methods of contraception have succeeded (Basu 1994).

Knowledge of the environment is itself a form of human capital. Environmental education can be particularly important in situations where people confront new environments, or where they face radically new stresses in old ones (Segura and Boyce 1994). By improving natural resource management by the poor, education can help to reduce some kinds of environmental degradation by the poor, and can enhance their ability to contest other types. The latter effect comes about for two reasons. First, education can improve knowledge of environmental costs, whose impacts and sources otherwise remain obscure. It is one thing to know that your child is sick, but something else to trace that sickness to a specific source of environmental contamination. Second, education can improve knowledge of how to wage successful political struggles – how to lobby government officials, initiate legal actions and mobilize public opinion. In summary, by providing environmental knowledge to people with an incentive to use it, education can alter the balance of power and thereby tilt environmental outcomes towards greater protection for natural capital.

Empirical Approaches to Resource Management and Environmental Policy: Some Examples

A Case Study of
Mangrove Management Options in Bintuni Bay, Irian Jaya, Indonesia

In order to determine an optimal resource management strategy, it is important to analyse both the market and non-market costs and benefits associated with linked resource uses of the resource, and how these costs and benefits are distributed among different sectors of the population over time. The results of such an analysis will depend on what assumptions are made about links between different resource uses. Improper management in forestry, for example, can result in significant economic losses in offshore fisheries. Economic analysis based on this consideration would lead to management recommendations for lower rates of conversion and exploitation, and generally demonstrate that some level of 'conservation' makes economic sense.

A study of management options for mangroves in Bintuni Bay, Irian Jaya in Indonesia, by Ruitenbeek (1991) demonstrated that (1) non-market traditional uses of mangroves are significant; (2) traditional mangrove use contributes proportionately more to low-income households; and (3) expansion in the wage economy will not be directly offset by decreased traditional reliance on mangroves.

The Bay supports an important shrimp export industry, and coastal areas support some 3,000 households in a mixed economy of farming, wages and traditional mangrove uses. Pressures from a woodchip export industry pose a direct threat to the mangrove ecosystem. Recent interest in the area has led to a proposed Bintuni Bay Nature Reserve, which would protect approximately 267,000 hectares of the ecosystem, 60,000 hectares of which is in the Bay itself.

The study consisted of a household survey to quantify the value of traditional uses of mangroves in the Bintuni Bay area; correlation studies of the 'economic linkages' between the formal sector economy and the traditional economy; and a cost-benefit analysis of different management options for the forestry component of the mangrove resource that incorporated different assumptions of 'ecological linkages' in order to capture some of the uncertainty inherent in ecosystem behaviour.

The total value of household income from marketed and non-marketed sources is about Rp9 million/yr/household ($4,500/yr/household), of which about 70% can be attributed to traditional non-commercial uses. Figure 1 shows that for the region as a whole, traditional uses from hunting, fishing and gathering account for a value of about Rp20 billion/yr ($10 million/yr). By comparison, commercial fisheries are valued at about Rp70 billion/yr ($35 million/yr) and selective commercial mangrove cutting schemes have a maximum value of about Rp40 billion/yr ($20 million/yr) – see Fig. 1.

FIGURE 1

Estimated Value of Household Production at Local Prices (x Rp1000/YEAR/HOUSEHOLD)

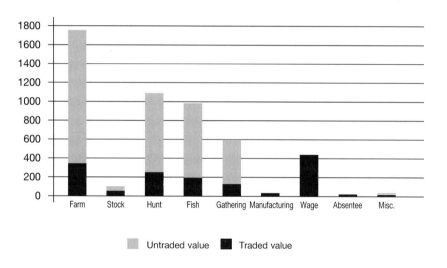

The actual sources of income (at local prices) are also shown in Figure 1. The value of production from the mangrove areas (traditional fishing, hunting and gathering) exceeds that from both cultivated crops and from formal sector wage income. A key observation from the household survey was that transfers arising from compensation payments from commercial forestry or fishing operations were very small; they represented less than 2% of cash income to the household.

An analysis of income inequality, and factors that contribute to it, demonstrated that there would be little 'trickle down effect' as a result of increased formal sector wage activity. Income inequality is comparable to that in most developing countries, but formal sector activities in the Bintuni Bay area would increase it, while hunting and gathering activities tend to decrease it because traditional mangrove use contributes proportionately more to low income households. Absolute levels of mangrove use are, however, substantial even for richer families. Fishing and farming have no significant effect on income inequality. The household data also showed that, although women comprise 50% of the population, they are responsible for only 22% of the cash income to the household. Most of their productive output, as shown in Figure 1, is related to products from farming and gathering. When this output is valued at local prices, women's production represents 49% of total output, which suggests that women play an important and equal economic role in the total production process.

An econometric analysis that correlated income sources with traditional uses of mangroves found that, although there is some substitution between activity in the formal and in the traditional sectors, a 10% expansion in the formal sector would only decrease traditional uses by 3%. The implication is that traditional mangrove use will continue to be important in the region even if formal sector development occurs. Table 7 illustrates some of the uses and environmental functions of mangroves.

TABLE 7

Examples of Uses and Environmental Functions of Mangroves

Sustainable Production Functions
- Timber
- Firewood
- Woodchips
- Charcoal
- Fish
- Curstaceans
- Shellfish
- Tannins
- Nipa
- Medicine
- Honey
- Traditional hunting, fishing gathering
- Genetic resources

Regulatory or Carrier Functions
- Erosion prevention (shoreline)
- Erosion prevention (riverbanks)
- Storage & recycling of human waste & pollutants
- Maintenance of biodiversity
- Provision of migration habitat
- Provision of nursery grounds
- Provision of breeding grounds
- Nutrient supply
- Nutrient regeneration
- Coral reef maintenance & protection
- Habitat for indigenous people
- Recreation sites

Conversion Uses
- Industrial/urban land use
- Aquaculture
- Salt ponds
- Rice fields
- Plantations
- Mining
- Dam sites

Information Functions
- Spiritual & religious information
- Cultural & artistic inspiration
- Educational, historical & scientific information
- Potential information

The cost-benefit analysis evaluated six forestry options that ranged from 100% clear cutting to a complete cutting ban. The clear cut option was only found optimal if effects on other ecosystem components (based on scientific evidence undertaken elsewhere) are ignored. The cutting ban option is optimal when there are linear and immediate effects on other ecosystem components. Under a scenario with linear but delayed effects of five years, selective cutting of 25% of the mangrove has a present value of Rp70 billion ($35 million) greater than the clear cutting option, and only Rp3 billion ($1.5 million) greater than the cutting ban option.

When linkages between ecosystem components are not taken into account, or when mangrove cutting is left unregulated, mangrove resources will often be over-exploited. The existence of linkages between mangrove area and overall ecosystem productivity means that strong economic arguments can be made for conservative (and sustainable) mangrove clearing. In instances where strong ecological ties occur, severe restrictions on clearing activities will be economically optimal. This generic result will apply to many situations in Indonesia where resource development needs place conflicting demands on mangrove and other ecological resources.

In the Bintuni Bay area, the analysis provides additional rationale for setting aside some of the mangrove area in a conservation area. If strong ecological interactions exist, the analysis showed that the optimal amount of cutting was less than 25% of the harvestable area. Given the proposed area of the reserve and characteristics of the mangrove outside of the reserve, to achieve a 25% target for the area as a whole would require that cutting outside of the reserve not exceed 60% of the harvestable area. Even so, if further research shows that ecological interactions are quite strong and rapid, or if critical habitats are being disturbed, then it would be economically justified to reduce cutting below this 60% threshold.

It must be recognized that there is still considerable uncertainty in the dynamics of specific mangrove ecosystems. This study has demonstrated that if we know the nature of these interactions, an economically optimal strategy can be selected. The analysis also demonstrates that if we do not know the nature of the interactions, an incorrect guess can have substantial economic penalties. If, for example, we assume that there are weak, delayed interactions and select an 80% selective cut on that basis, and if it turns out that the actual interactions are immediate and strong, then the economic value of such a decision in the Bintuni Bay case would be about Rp500 billion ($250 million) less than what was expected, and Rp160 billion ($80 million) less than the optimal strategy. Such penalties are substantial; the entire GDP of Kabupaten Manokwari is estimated to be less than Rp100 billion ($50 million) annually. Decision-makers must be aware of what the potential losses of incorrect decisions might be – even when information is incomplete or uncertain – and act accordingly.

The current situation of uncertainty raises two further issues: (1) that there is a need for information relating to the linkages between ecosystem components; and (2) that policies which mitigate the effects of the linkages will have economic as well as ecological merit. Where ecosystem dynamics are uncertain, programmes reducing linkage effects – such as greenbelts, replanting or selective cutting – will minimize potential economic losses.

Finally, the study points out the importance of macro-economic policy linkages. Trade policy, fiscal policy, monetary policy, foreign exchange rate policy, and most other macro-economic policies, can have an effect on mangrove systems. A shrimp export subsidy would, for example, provide an incentive for increased shrimp trawling in mangrove areas. This might in turn disrupt traditional fisheries. Promoting woodchip exports could, similarly, increase mangrove cutting and thereby disrupt other components of the ecosystem through ecological linkages. A specific example is shown in Figure 2 to depict a potential scenario occurring in the South Sulawesi mangrove areas. Lowland taxes induce conversion to tambak which, through both ecological and socio-economic linkages, eventually causes degradation of near-shore fisheries.

FIGURE 2

An Example of Ecological Economic Linkages between Macro-policy and Local Ecosystem Effects

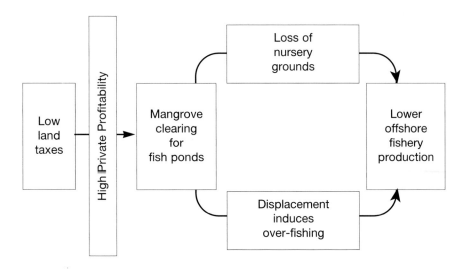

A Case Study of the
Impact of Pricing of Energy and Natural Resources in Spain

Full-cost pricing is an allocative mechanism that can be used to provide feedback to individuals about the relationship of resource use to production. Subsidies and unaccounted externalities remove that feedback to individuals and interfere with market mechanisms that might otherwise allocate resources more efficiently. One way to determine if an agricultural or other resource input is underpriced is to compare the price of an input, in proportion to the price of all inputs, to its energy cost in proportion to the energy cost of other inputs.

In a case study of agriculture in arid lands in Spain, for example, it was found that, in general, the energy cost of water used in irrigation was 40% of all energy costs. In contrast, water was only about 2% of the monetary costs and was causing salt pollution (see Table 8). It was concluded from this that water was underpriced and that, because of this subsidy, the farmer had little or no information about the value of water and the relation between water use and crop production. Because of this lack of information, no market mechanism was available to reduce salt pollution, and efforts to control pollution would instead require regulation.

If the price of water were instead raised to a level approximating its full cost, farmers might be motivated to shift towards crops which use less water and more closely allocate water to plant needs that would reduce salt pollution. Agronomists and hydrologists in Aragon felt that these practices could reduce water use by 20%.

TABLE 8

A Comparison of Energy and Monetary Data for the Production of a Crop of Maize on La Violada Landscape

Inputs	Energy MJ/Ha	Economics Pesetas/Ha
Irrigation water & ppt	29,535	3,000
Seeds	405	13,000
Fertilizer	37,722	46,333
Machinery (sequestered)	1,849	
Farming operations	10,018	10,500
Fuel	6,707	7,680
Pesticides	151	4,202
Total	**86,387**	**84,715**
Outputs		
Harvested product	218,252	212,500
Drainage water	701	
Evapotranspiration	30,472	

Energy is reported in million joules per hectare and the economic expenses and gains in Spanish pesetas per hectare. The data represent one crop period, not a full year.

Energy and Social Costs and Sectoral Development:
A Case Study in Agriculture

The large increases in the yields of the world's major grain crops in the last half century are often attributed to the Green Revolution, a shining example of the triumph of science over nature. But it is important to understand the biophysical basis of the Green Revolution, which is based on (1) the large subsidy of solar energy with non-renewable natural capital (fossil fuels) and human capital (tractors, plant breeding), and (2) the substitution of certain forms of renewable natural capital in agriculture (allelopathy, nutrient cycles) with non-renewable natural capital and manufactured capital (mechanized weed control, fertilizers). In essence, what we have done is re-allocate the work required to produce edible plant biomass between various forms of human and natural capital, with a lion's share of the work now being done by the non-renewable and human capital components.

There are significant consequences of substituting the work done by plants, a form of renewable natural capital, with non-renewable natural capital and human capital. Plants that are bred to respond to fossil fuel inputs become highly dependent on them for their success and survival. Traditional varieties evolve around, and are better adapted to, the environmental conditions of their region. High yield varieties (HYV) are adapted to inputs of fertilizers, mechanization and other fossil fuel-based inputs across many different regions. As a result, HYV of cultivars are frequently inferior to traditional varieties under low-input conditions. In many developing nations without access to sufficient amounts or types of energy subsidies (fertilizers, irrigation), yields are far below the levels achieved in the industrial world. Another consequence is that the total energy cost of plant production in industrial agro-ecosystems is much higher than natural systems.

In a comparison of the ratio of energy inputs to outputs in maize production in different countries, it was found that the United States had the lowest ratio of all inputs to yield (2.9) compared to, for example, Mexico, which had 12.5. The United States, however, had the highest output per amount of human effort (4,233-5,926) compared with 13.9 for Mexico. Pimentel also shows that over twice as much energy is consumed to till a hectare of soil using a 50-hp tractor as would be used by human labour.

The large flow of energy, materials and environmental services through agro-ecosystems is mirrored by the depletion and degradation of many types and quantities of natural capital at a variety of spatial scales. The environmental impact of industrial agriculture can be categorized generally as impacts that deplete non-renewable natural capital, and impacts that deplete or degrade renewable natural capital.

Foremost among these impacts is the fact that food production for a large and increasing fraction of the world's population is now driven principally by stock resources instead of flow resources, i.e., non-renewable natural capital rather than renewable natural capital. In populous nations such as India, unsubsidized solar energy cannot generate a sufficient quality and quantity of calories to sustain that nation's 890 million people (and growing at 2.07% per year). Stocks of crude oil, natural gas and phosphate rock are depleted to produce the fuel, fertilizers and other inputs necessary to sustain the level of productivity that many nations now depend on. The dependence on stock resources ensures that the energy cost of those inputs, and hence the cost of the food grown with them, will rise as the energy costs of extracting oil and phosphate increase with their depletion. The dependence on oil and gas also ties the financial plight of many farmers to the world price of oil, which is unstable and unpredictable. The energy price shocks in recent decades had an enormous economic impact on farmers throughout the world. Combined with stable or falling grain prices, the energy price shocks precipitated the United States farm crisis in the 1980s, and had a devastating impact on farms that used large amounts of energy to pump groundwater in arid regions of the nation.

Renewable natural capital is converted to a non-renewable form when it is used or degraded at a rate faster than it is regenerated by natural processes. Examples of that process are soil erosion, soil degradation and groundwater mining. The rate of soil erosion in most agro-ecosystems in the world is substantially greater than the rate of soil formation. Row cropping, the elimination of fallow periods, mechanization, the extension of cultivation to marginal lands, the harvest of crop residues and other factors intensify soil erosion. Similarly, irrigation effectively mines underground water in regions where withdrawal exceeds the natural recharge. Water quality is significantly impaired in regions where soil erosion is high and where agricultural chemicals are washed into surface waters or leached into groundwater.

The human response to the depletion of agricultural natural capital often accelerates or reinforces the existing problem, both in agriculture and in other sectors of the economy. To maintain crop yields, the reduction of soil fertility caused by erosion requires an increase in fertilizer application to maintain production. In fact, about 50% of the fertilizer applied to United States farmland simply replaces nutrients lost by soil erosion. This establishes a positive feedback loop between soil erosion and the stocks of crude oil and phosphate rock. The increase in fertilizer use requires the mining of more natural gas and phosphate rock to replace the nitrogen and phosphorous that wash from the soil. The extraction of natural gas and phosphate rock accelerates the depletion of the remaining stocks of those resources which, in turn, increases the energy and resource cost of natural gas and phosphate. In fact, the energy cost to extract a cubic foot of natural gas and a ton of phosphate rock is increasing (Cleveland 1991), so their use to offset soil depletion simply accelerates their energy cost, and thereby the indirect energy cost of the crops grown on the depleted soil.

Another example of this positive feedback system is the depletion of groundwater. The exploitation of groundwater for irrigation and municipal purposes at rates greater than the rate of recharge has caused sharp declines in the water level in many United States aquifers and other regions. The energy cost of lifting water is a direct function of depth to water level. Thus, the depletion of groundwater natural capital initiates a positive feedback loop in which more energy is extracted to lift the same quantity of water a greater distance, which depletes fossil fuel resources, which in turn enhances the increase in the energy cost of pumping, and so on.

A third example of the positive feedback between the depletion of natural capital, energy use and human response is pest control. Control of pests and diseases with human-directed energy is essential in industrial agriculture because the natural self-defence mechanisms of most crops have been altered or erased through plant breeding and agronomic practices, and because the reduced diversity of monocultures automatically makes them easier targets for pests and diseases. But pesticides frequently eliminate a critical form of natural capital – the 'free' pest control provided by the natural system, mostly through predacious insects that feed on the pests. Insect pests are generally less susceptible to pesticides than are their predators, and their populations tend to be large. As a result, natural predators are eradicated more rapidly than the target pest species, and the latter develop resistance to the pesticides. The number of insects that are resistant to at least one pesticide is increasing rapidly (Bull 1982). Pest control can only be maintained by spraying larger amounts of pesticides, or by scientists in the agrochemical industry trying to stay one step ahead of the evolving pests by developing more exotic and lethal chemicals. Of course, most of those chemicals are derivatives of crude oil, so the depletion of natural defence mechanisms and the race against the mutations of pest insects put us back on the same resource depletion treadmill.

Soil erosion in many developing nations is much worse than in industrial nations because population pressure forces cultivation on to increasingly marginal, and hence highly erodible lands, while at the same time intensive, fossil fuel-based monocultures are encouraged by host governments and international lending agencies. The situation is exacerbated by the increasing tendency of the rural poor to collect and burn crop residues for cooking and heating. About one-third of the biomass fuel in the world is now crop residues (David Pimentel, personal communication). Removal of the residues accelerates erosion because they form an important protective cover for the soil surface (Pimentel *et al.* 1981). China averages soil erosion of about 43 t/ha/yr (tonnes per hectare per year), and Zimbabwe about 50 t/ha/yr, compared to 16 t/ha/yr in the United States and compared to the soil formation rate of approximately 1 t/ha/yr (Pimentel *et al.* 1987).

In India, for example, about 6 billion tonnes of soil are eroded each year.

Estimates of the average rate of erosion vary from 7 to 75 t/ha/yr, with many estimates falling in the range of 30 to 40 t/ha/yr (see Table 9). Some of the highest rates of erosion are on the fertile soils in northeastern India. These rates are extraordinarily fast compared with the slow rate of natural soil formation. Many interrelated factors contribute to soil erosion in India. Most of the 24 million hectares of new agricultural land brought under cultivation from 1951 to the mid-1980s was marginal, highly erodible soil. Deforestation of watersheds increases run-off and thereby accelerates erosion and flooding on agricultural and other types of land. The catastrophic deforestation and erosion problems in the Himalayan watersheds are legendary. Deforestation also reduces the supply of fuelwood, causing the increased harvest of crop residues for fuel, which accelerates erosion. The combined effects of deforestation and erosion have many deleterious results. Fertilizer use increases to replace lost nutrients. Throughout all of India, the land area subject to annual flooding tripled between 1960 and 1984, and is now equivalent to more than 20% of the entire land area. Sedimentation rates in the catchment areas of some of India's major reservoirs are three to four times the predicted rates, and may shorten considerably the useful life of those reservoirs.

Soil conservation programmes are underway to combat the problem. Prime Minister Rajiv Gandhi established the National Wastelands Development Board in 1985 to address the general problem of land degradation, and to restore some highly eroded lands. By the end of the Sixth Five Year Plan, about 29.4 million hectares were covered under some type of soil conservation programme. There are, however, severe barriers to the adoption of such programmes, not the least of which is the fact that a large majority of Indian farmers are extremely poor, lack sufficient capital to invest in conservation programmes, and do not have ready access to the technological and communication infrastructure that disseminates the conservation programmes. Moreover, the poorer farmers hold much of the marginal, erosion-prone land, on which yields are already extremely low. The marginal decline in yields due to erosion is likely to be very small in these cases, increasing the reticence of the farmers towards soil conservation (Venkateswarlu 1985).

The pattern of water use has significantly impaired the land and water resource base in India and, as a result, poses a serious challenge to one of the most heavily irrigated agricultural systems in the world. Groundwater depletion is a serious problem in many regions, where withdrawals now exceed recharge. Overdrafts accelerated in the 1970s when tube wells powered by diesel engines and electric motors rapidly replaced open dug wells. The adoption of tube wells was encouraged by financial assistance for mechanized water withdrawal systems. Individual case studies are representative of the national problem. The water table in large parts of Tamil Nadu fell 25 to 30 metres in the 1970s (Jayal 1985). In

TABLE 9

Estimates of Recent Soil Erosion Rates in India

Study	Region or soil type	Erosion rate tonnes per hectare per year	Comments
Pimentel *et al.* 1987	national average	25-30	assumes 6 billion tonnes lost per year, 60-70% on cultivated land
	Deccan black soil region	40-100	
Narayana and Sastry 1985	national average for red soils	4-10	sheet erosion on 72 million hectares
	national average for black soils	11-43	sheet erosion on 88 million hectares
	national average	>33	gulley erosion on 4 million hectares
	national average	>80	hill erosion on 13 million hectares
Venkateswarlu 1985	national average	7	
	Upper Gangetic alluvial plains	3	
	Lower Gangetic alluvial plains	14	
	Assam Valley	28	
	Western coastal region	39	

Maharashtra, 77 out of 1,481 watersheds have rates of withdrawal that exceed rates of recharge (Jayal 1985). In that region, competition for limited water supplies has developed between local subsistence farmers and larger farms that grow heavily watered commercial crops such as sugarcane. According to some experts India is losing land from irrigation mismanagement at the same rate as land is being put into irrigation. The cost of providing additional irrigation now is much higher, because all easily irrigable areas were brought into production by the 1980s. Alkalinity, salinity and waterlogging increase and affect productivity directly, because of the lack of drainage. Forty per cent more inputs were needed in 1989 for the same amount of production as in 1970. The need for inputs and pesticides is still growing at the rate of 8.5% a year. Over 60 different elements are needed by plants, but only 3 are replenished in fertilization. Excessive fertilizer application in high growth

Green Revolution regions also affects soil microbial properties, apart from the fact that it stimulates weed growth. Monocultures mine the nutrients in the top layer of soil and interfere with the flow of nutrients between layers of soil. Sixty per cent of pesticides in India are used on cotton and have a treadmill effect because they also kill predators. The average consumption of pesticides and fertilizers is low but locally concentrated. In the Gunter district, for example, pesticide use is equivalent to that of Japan, which is ten times the United States level of use. In Andra Pradesh, several families pawned jewelry to invest in pesticide inputs that did not work. When the crop failed, the families committed suicide.

The poor ecosystem management strategies that evolved in industrial agriculture set in motion a series of complex modifications and feedbacks that have depleted the renewable and non-renewable natural capital basis of food production. The consequences of that depletion were less significant when fertile land and high quality fossil fuel deposits were abundant, and when population demands were small. The situation today demands new strategies for supplying food to a growing population. Cheap oil is a principal barrier to the implementation of new strategies, because it can be used in the short run to mask the long-term effects of the depletion of other forms of natural capital. The good news is that many of the components of sustainable agriculture do not require massive technical innovation. Indeed, reducing the depletion of natural capital in agriculture will require a return to many forms of human capital that guide traditional agriculture. Practices such as intercropping, polyculture, biological pest control, traditional shifting cultivation, and agroforestry are based on centuries of experience of producing food in ways that maintain the natural capital basis of agriculture. Appropriate economic and institutional incentives that will guide agriculture towards these practices are required, while ensuring the production of sufficient food to meet the world's growing population (Cleveland 1991).

Industrial agriculture also displaced smallholder and traditional agriculture systems, because it was assumed that production efficiency was related to farm size and that smallholders were inefficient and expensive. The displacement of smallholders by industrialized corporate farms was also made possible by special advantages being made available to large growers such as agricultural support programmes, tax policies, and agricultural labour policies, as well as the externalization of environmental and social costs.

In a recent review of the literature pertaining to smallholder agriculture Netting (1993) found that, in general, the efficiency of small farms was equal to or greater than large farms in terms of cost per unit of output. Medium- and small-sized farms also had the advantage of maximizing employment, total production, trade and income (Goldschmidt 1978) as well as being more diversified and spending less on inputs. The long-run returns also provide for security in less developed countries, where there are no state welfare benefits or company pensions. Smallholder intensive agriculture may provide an economic stimulus through its capacity for absorbing labour as well as providing a multiplier effect throughout the economy. Rural communities based on smallholder agriculture also had a higher quality of life as measured by higher average family income, number of stores and amount of retail trade, number of schools, parks and newspapers and the quality of streets. The rural communities that were in decline were those that had an increase in farm size rather than a fall in production because migrant labourers, foremen and equipment drivers did not provide the base for stable communities. 'Everyone who has done careful research on farm size, residency of agricultural landowners and social conditions in the rural community finds the same relationship: as farm size and absentee ownership increase, social conditions in the local community deteriorate.' (Dean MacCannell, quoted in Strange 1988; Netting 1993). Smallholders also have more stewardship incentives in order to pass on their source of livelihood to the next generation. Netting (1993) concludes that '...their experience, their fertile land, their livestock, and their diversified production strategies [provide] a set of defenses against the uncontrollable vagaries of weather, prices, and war. Smallholders may not always live well, but they are seasoned survivors. They may moonlight as craftsmen, petty traders, field hands, or factory workers, but they do not keep one foot on the farm out of sentiment or stupidity. And the society that dispossesses smallholders in favour of factory farms, plantations, or socialistic communes simultaneously risks a decline in agricultural production, rural unemployment, and ecological deterioration.... Where people are plentiful and land is scarce, the distinctive adaptation of smallholder households practicing intensive agriculture will appear, just as it has for centuries in a variety of human societies.'

We add that the same would probably apply to artisanal fisheries. They would be expected to have more flexibility for adjusting to fluctuations in resource availability as well as to support a social structure conducive to cooperation in the management and conservation of the resource. The preservation of rural 'working landscapes' and human-scale of activities is not only more likely to meet human needs but also to be compatible with ecosystem approaches to resource management and long-term sustainability.

Costs and Benefits of Environmental Restoration in an Urban Squatter Settlement: a Case Study in Rio de Janeiro

A valuation of measures for environmental restoration in the critical zones of the hillside squatter settlements or *favelas* in Rio de Janeiro is focusing on the inhabitants of the *favelas*, who are the prime beneficiaries of these investments, in order to identify their priorities and aspirations, and make popular participation and implementation more effective. It is also being used to demonstrate the benefits of these projects to the municipal government so that they may be appropriately prioritized.

The project was part of a series of actions taken in 25 communities by the municipal government of Rio to urbanize the *favelas*, particularly those situated in areas of risk. These *favelas* are characterized by steep slopes, poor soils and the lack of defined property rights. The most serious problem was homelessness resulting from mudslides and falling boulders during the torrential rains that occur from summer to autumn. People move there, however, because they will be close to opportunities for work. Also, the visibility of the *favela* communities gives them more political power to obtain government services, such as water, sanitation, electricity and documentation of property rights. There were also effects on the urban population living below the *favelas*.

The main objective of the project was to minimize problems that occurred from unplanned occupation in ecologically fragile areas, to restore vegetation on eroded hillsides and reduce the possibility of accidents due to landslides, flooding and inundation. The project was also designed to make use of manual labour, to provide local remuneration and to count on the participation of the inhabitants in its implemention.

The reforestation, and the drainage works associated with it, has, in fact, reduced the quantity of sediment carried and deposited in the period of most intense rainfall, probably reducing the risks of inundation to the people situated at the base of the hill. The calculations done so far indicate that the consequent avoidance of damage and increased property values exceed the cost of the municipal investment, and justify the expenditure of public resources for environmental restoration. To legitimize the expenditure however, these investments must also be valued according to the costs and benefits derived by the target population. A second phase of the work is evaluating the implementation of the project, and the effectiveness of public interventions on the needs and aspirations of the inhabitants. In addition to providing a detailed and precise analysis of the case in its variable relationships with the biophysical environment, the study seeks to identify and analyse socio-economic variables that can be used to identify other sources of value, quantified or not, that are perceived by the inhabitants of São Jose Operario and in the adjacent communities. From the community perspective, the highest priority is sanitation. Reforestation was seen as limiting space for growth although the inhabitants favoured the drainage benefits. They also expressed a preference for fruit trees. Sources of environmental degradation, the distribution of effects and mitigation measures are outlined in Table 10.

TABLE 10

Sources of Degradation, Environmental Effects, Recipients and Interventions by City Hall of the Municipality of Rio de Janeiro on the Hill of São Jose Operario, Jacarepagua

Sources of degradation	Effects of intervention	Recipients	Interventions
Granite mining	Erosion/ sedimentation	Ecosystem/ watershed	Mining prohibition
	Flooding	Collective infrastructure	Containment of hillsides and rock outcroppings
	Risk of rockfall/ mudslide	Homes/ improvements	Drainage works
		Downstream community	
Lack of basic infrastructure	Health costs	Local population, particularly children (previous high incidence of diarrhoea)	Storm sewerage works
	High cost of service provision (water supply, waste disposal)		Paving
			Trash removal/ recycling

REFERENCES AND FURTHER READING

Abramovitz, J.N., and R. Nichols 1992. 'Women and biodiversity: ancient reality, modern imperative'. *Development* 1992:2.

Agarwal, A., and S. Narain 1991. 'Global warming in an unequal world'. *International Journal of Sustainable Development* 1 (1):98-104.

Anderson, A.B., P.H. May and M.J. Balick 1991. *The Subsidy from Nature. Palm Forests, Peasantry, and Development on an Amazon Frontier.* New York: Columbia University Press.

Annis, S. 1992. *Poverty, Natural Resources and Public Policy in Central America.* New Brunswick: Transaction Publishers.

Ardayfio-Schandorf, E. 1993. 'Household energy supply and women's work in Ghana'. In *Different Places, Different Voices: Gender and Development in Africa, Asia, and Latin America*, eds J. H. Momsen and V. Kinnard. London, New York: Routledge.

Arizpe, L., R. Costanza and W. Lutz 1991. 'Population and natural resource use'. In *An Agenda of Science for Environment and Development into the 21st Century*, eds J.C.I. Dooge *et al.* Cambridge: Cambridge University Press.

Arntzen, J. 1994. 'Population dynamics, economic development and environmental changes in developing countries'. Mimeo.

Arntzen, J. 1989. *Environmental Pressure and Adaptation in Rural Botswana.* Amsterdam: Free University.

Bacon, K.H. 1993. 'Clinton looks to a bank in Bangladesh for model to help U.S. poor get loans'. *Wall Street Journal*, 29 August 1993.

Bailey, C. 1988. 'The social consequences of tropical shrimp mariculture development'. *Ocean and Shoreline Management* 11:31-44.

Bakkes, J.A., G.J. van den Born, J.C. Helder, R.J. Swart, C.W. Hope and J.D.E Parker 1994. *An Overview of Environmental Indicators: State of the Art and Perspectives.* Report to UNEP, UNEP/RIVM, Nairobi.

Barbier, E.B. and J.C. Burgess 1993. 'Timber trade and tropical deforestation. Global trends and evidence from Indonesia'. Paper presented at the Northeast Universities Development Consortium Conference, Williams College, Williamstown, Massachusetts, 15-16 October 1993.

Barker, C. 1992. 'Strategic issues for the GEF'. Paper, World Resources Institute, Washington, D.C., November 1992.

Barnard, G.W. 1987. *Woodfuel in Developing Countries*. Chichester: John Wiley and Sons.

Barraclough, S., and K. Ghimire 1990. 'The social dynamics of deforestation in developing countries'. Discussion Paper No. 16. Geneva: United Nations Research Institute for Social Development.

Barrie, L.A., D. Gregor, B. Hargrave, R. Lake, D. Muir, R. Shearer, B. Tracey and T. Bidleman 1992. 'Arctic contaminants: sources, occurrence and pathways'. *The Science of the Total Environment* 122:1-74.

Bartelmus, P. 1994. *A Framework for Indicators of Sustainable Development*. New York: United Nations Department for Economic and Social Information and Policy Analysis.

Bartelmus, P., E. Lutz and S. Schweinfest 1992. 'Integrated environmental and economic accounting: a case study for Papua New Guinea'. World Bank Environment Department Working Paper No. 54. Washington, D.C.: The World Bank.

Basu, A. 1994. 'The status of woman and demographic change'. Background Paper, Second India Reassessment Study. Delhi: Institute of Economic Growth.

Ben Abdallah, T., and P. Engelhard 1993. 'The urgency of fighting poverty, for democracy and the environment'. Occasional Paper. Geneva: United Nations Non-Governmental Liaison Service.

Blakie, M., and B. Brookfield 1987. *Land Degradation and Society*. London: Methuen.

Bongaarts, J. 1994. 'Population policy options in the developing world'. *Science* 263:771-6.

Brinley, T. 1961. *International Migration and Economic Development*. New York: UNESCO.

Briscoe, J. 1993. 'When the cup is half full: improving water and sanitation services in the developing world'. *Environment* 35:4.

Brown, H. 1954. *The Challenge of Man's Future*. New York: The Viking Press.

Brown, L.R., and J.E. Young 1990. 'Feeding the world in the nineties'. In *Feeding the World in the Nineties*, ed. L.R. Brown. New York: W.W. Norton

Brush, S. 'Genetic diversity and conservation in traditional farming systems'. *Journal of Ethnobiology* 6:1.

Bull, D. 1982. *A Growing Problem: Pesticides and the Third World*. Oxfam: Oxford University Press.

Bunker, S.G. 1985. *Underdeveloping the Amazon: Extraction, Unequal Exchange, and the Failure of the Modern State*. Chicago: University of Chicago Press.

Cairncross, F. 1993. *Costing the Earth: The Challenge for Governments, the Opportunities for Business*. Boston: Harvard Business School Press.

Caldwell, J. 1982. *The Theory of Fertility Decline*. New York: Academic Press.

Campbell, T. 1989. 'Urban development in the Third World: environmental dilemmas and the urban poor'. In *Environment and the Poor: Development Strategies for a Common Agenda*, eds J.H. Leonard *et al.* Overseas Development Council, U.S.-Third World Policy Perspectives, No. 11. New Brunswick: Transaction Books.

Cassen, R.H. 1976. 'Population and development: a survey'. *World Development* 4 (10/11): 785-830.

Cernea, M.M. 1993. 'The building blocks of participation: testing bottom-up planning'. World Bank Discussion Paper 166. Washington, D.C.: The World Bank.

Chambers, R. 1988. 'Sustainable livelihoods, environment and development: putting poor rural people first'. Discussion Paper 240. Brighton: Institute of Development Studies, University of Sussex.

Chopra, K., and G.K. Kadekodi 1991, 'Participatory institutions: the context of common and private property resources'. *Resource and Environmental Economics* 1 (4):353-372.

Chopra, K., Kadekodi, G.K., and Murty, M.N. 1990. *Participatory Development, People and Common Property Resources*. New Delhi: Sage Publications.

Chopra, K., and C.H.H. Rao 1992. 'The links between sustainable growth and poverty'. *Journal of International Agriculture* 31(4):364-79.

CIDIE 1993. *Implications of Agenda 21 for the Committee of International Development Institutions on the Environment (CIDIE) and Proposed Activities*. Washington, D.C.: Committee of International Development Institutions on the Environment.

—. 1993. *Basic Information on Activities Undertaken by CIDIE Members on Environment Related Matters*. Washington, D.C.: Committee of International Development Institutions on the Environment.

—. 1992. *Status and Role of the Commission on Sustainable Development (CSD) and its relationship with the activities of CIDIE members*. Washington, D.C.: Committee of International Development Institutions on the Environment.

—. 1992. *CIDIE Summary Record*. Washington, D.C.: Committee of International Development Institutions on the Environment.

—. 1992. *Consolidated Report on Activities in the Implementation of the Declaration of Environmental Policies and Procedures Relating to Economic Development.* Washington, D.C.: Committee of International Development Institutions on the Environment.

—. 1991. *Conclusions of the High Level Meeting of the Committee of International Development Institutions on the Environment (Twelfth CIDIE Meeting).* Washington, D.C.: Committee of International Development Institutions on the Environment.

Clark, C. 1958. 'Population growth and living standards'. In *The Economics of Underdevelopment*, eds A.M. Agarwala and S.P. Singh. London: Oxford University Press.

Clarke, R. 1993. *Water: The International Crisis.* Cambridge, MA: MIT Press.

Cleveland, C.J. 1991. 'Natural resource scarcity and economic growth revisited: economics and biophysical perspectives'. In *Ecological Economics: The Science and Management of Sustainability*, ed. R. Costanza. New York: Columbia University Press.

—. 1993. 'Re-allocating work between human and natural capital in agriculture'. In *Investing in Natural Capital: The Ecological Economics Approach to Sustainability*, eds A.-M. Jansson, C. Folke, M. Hammer and R. Costanza. Washington, D.C.: ISEE/Island Press.

Corden, W.M. 1974. *Trade Policy and Economic Welfare.* Oxford: Clarendon Press.

Costanza, R. 1994. 'Three general policies to achieve sustainability'. In *Investing in Natural Capital: The Ecological Economics Approach to Sustainability*, eds A.-M. Jansson, C. Folke, R. Costanza and M. Hammer. Washington, D.C.: ISEE/Island Press.

—. 1993. *The Social Costs of Energy Use in Ecological Economic Systems.* Report prepared for the U.S. Congress, Office of Technology Assessment. Solomons, MD: MIIEE.

—. ed. 1991. *Ecological Economics: The Science and Management of Sustainability.* New York: Columbia University Press.

—. 1987. 'Social traps and environmental policy'. *BioScience* 37:407-12.

Costanza, R., and H.E. Daly 1992. 'Natural capital and sustainable development'. *Conservation Biology* V 6(1).

Cox, S. 1992. *Poverty, Natural Resources and Public Policy in Central America.* New Brunswick: Transaction Publishers.

Cross, J.G., and M.J. Guyer 1980. *Social Traps*. Ann Arbor: University of Michigan Press.

Daly, H. 1992. 'Allocation, distribution, and scale: towards an economics that is efficient, just, and sustainable'. *Ecological Economics* 6:185-93.

Daly, H.E., and J.B. Cobb, Jr. 1989. *For the Common Good: Redirecting the Economy Toward Community, the Environment, and a Sustainable Future*. Boston: Beacon.

Daly, H.E., and Goodland, R. 1995. 'An ecological-economic assessment of deregulation of international commerce under GATT'. *Ecological Economics*. In press.

Dasgupta, P. 1993. *An Inquiry into Well-Being and Destitution*. New York: Oxford University Press.

Dasgupta, P., and K. Maler 1991. *The Environment and the Emerging Development Issues: The Proceedings of the World Bank Annual Conference on Development Economics*. Washington D.C.: The World Bank.

Demeny, P. 1988. 'Demography and the limits of growth'. In *Population and Development Review Supplement* 14:213-44.

Duchin, F., and G.M. Lange 1994. 'Strategies for environmentally sound economic development'. In *Investing in Natural Capital: The Ecological Economics Approach to Sustainaiblity*, eds A.-M. Jansson, C. Folke, R. Costanza and M. Hammer. Washington, D.C.: ISEE/Island Press.

Duke, J.A. 1992. 'Tropical botanical extractives'. In *Sustainable Harvest and Marketing of Rain Forest Products*, eds M. Plotkin and L. Famolare. Washington, D.C.: Island Press.

Durning, A.B. 1989. 'Poverty and the environment: reversing the downward spiral'. Worldwatch Paper No. 92. Washington, D.C.: Worldwatch Institute.

Durning, A. 1991. 'Asking how much is enough'. In *State of the World*, eds L.R. Brown *et al*. A Worldwatch Institute Report on Progress Toward a Sustainable Development. Washington, D.C.: Worldwatch Institute.

Ehrlich, P.R., and A.E. Ehrlich 1991. *Healing the Planet*. Reading: Addison Wesley.

Ekins, P., and M. Max-Neef, eds 1992. *Real-Life Economics: Understanding Wealth Creation*. London: Routledge.

Ekins, P., C. Folke and R. Costanza 1995. 'Trade, environment, and development: the issues in perspective'. *Ecological Economics*. In press.

El-Ashry, M.T. 1993. 'Remarks of the Chairman of the Global Environment Facility'. Washington, D.C.: Global Environment Facility, 13 November 1993.

Erikson, K. 1994. *A New Species of Trouble. Explorations in Disaster, Trauma, and Community*. New York: W.W. Norton.

Evans, L.T. 1980. 'The natural history of crop yields'. *American Scientist* 68:388-97.

Faci, J., R. Aragues, F. Albert, D. Quilez, J. Machin and J.L. Arrue 1984. 'Water and salt balance in an irrigated area of the Ebro River Basin (Spain)'. *Irrigation Science* 6:1-9.

Falkenmark, M., and G. Lindh 1993. 'Water and economic development'. In *Water in Crisis: A Guide to the World's Fresh Water Resources*, ed. P.H. Gleick. Pacific Institute for Studies in Development, Environment, and Security. Stockholm Environment Institute. New York, Oxford: Oxford University Press.

FAO 1993. *Strategies for Sustainable Agriculture and Rural Development: The Role of Agriculture, Forestry and Fisheries*. Rome: United Nations Food and Agriculture Organization.

—. 1993. 'Rural poverty alleviation: policies and trends'. FAO Economic and Social Development Paper, 113. Rome: United Nations Food and Agriculture Organization.

—. 1992. 'Empowering the rural poor: FAO experiences in participatory rural development'. Rome: United Nations Food and Agriculture Organization.

—. 1984. 'Land, food and people'. Rome: United Nations Food and Agriculture Organization.

Findlay, R. 1970. *Trade and Specialization*. Harmondsworth: Penguin.

—. 1987. 'Comparative advantage'. In *The New Palgrave: a Dictionary of Economics*, Vol. 1, eds J. Eatwell, M. Milgate and P. Newman. London: Macmillan.

Foy, G., and H.E. Daly 1989. 'Allocation, distribution and scale as determinants of environmental degradation: case studies of Haiti, El Salvador and Costa Rica'. Environment Department Working Paper No. 19. Washington, D.C.: The World Bank.

Gallopin, G.C., P. Gutman and H. Maletta 1989. 'Global impoverishment, sustainable development and the environment: a conceptual approach'. *International Social Science Journal* (August): 121.

GEF 1992. *Global Environment Facility: A Bulletin on the Global Environment Facility*, No. 7, December 1992. Washington, D.C.: Global Environment Facility.

—. 1993. 'Terms of reference: evaluation of the Global Environment Facility pilot phase', 1083 08, February 24, 1993. Washington, D.C.: Global Environment Facility.

Gibbs, C.J.N., and D.W. Bromley 1989. 'Institutional arrangements for management of rural resources: common property regimes'. In *Common Property Resources*, ed. F. Berkes. London: Belhaven.

Githingi, M., and C. Perrings 1993. 'Social and ecological sustainability in the use of biotic resources in sub-Saharan Africa'. *Ambio* 22(2-3):110-16.

Goldschmidt, W. 1978. *As You Sow: Three Studies in the Social Consequences of Agribusiness*. Montclair, NJ: Allanheld, Osmun & Co.

Golley, F. 1995. *Rebuilding a Humane and Ethical Decision System for Investing in Natural Capital*. In press.

Goodland, R., and H. Daly 1993. 'Poverty alleviation is essential for environmental sustainability'. World Bank Environment Department Divisional Working Paper No. 1993-42. Washington, D.C.: The World Bank.

—. 1993. 'Why Northern income growth is not the solution to Southern poverty'. World Bank Environment Department Divisional Working Paper No. 1993-43. Washington, D.C.: The World Bank.

Greenaway, D., Bleaney, M., and Stewart, I.M.T., eds 1991. *Companion to Contemporary Economic Thought*. London: Routledge.

Guppy, N. 1984. 'Tropical deforestation: a global view'. *Foreign Affairs* 62 (4):928-65.

Gupta, A.K. 1993. 'Sustainable institutions for natural resource management: how do we participate in people's plans?' Indian Institute of Management, Ahmedabad. Unpublished draft.

—. 1992. 'Eco-institutional perspective on maintaining diversity'. Indian Institute of Management, Ahmedabad. Working paper.

—. 1990. 'Portfolio theory of technological change: reconceptualising farming systems research'. Indian Institute of Management, Ahmedabad. Working paper.

—. 1989. 'The design of resource-delivery systems: a socio-ecological perspective'. *International Studies of Management and Organisation* 18(4):64-82.

—. 1985a. 'Socio-ecological paradigm for analyzing problems of poor in dry regions'. *Ecodevelopment News* (Paris) No. 32-33, March 1985:68-74.

—. 1985b. 'On organising equity: are solutions really the problem?' *Journal of Social and Economic Studies* 2 (4):295-312.

—. 1985c. 'Socio-ecology of stress: why do common property resource management projects fail? – a case study of sheep and pasture development projects in Rajasthan, India'. Paper presented at the Conference on Management of CPR, National Academy of Sciences, BOSTID, US, Annapolis, 21-26 April 1985. Proceedings published by National Research Council, Washington, D.C., 305-22.

—. 1981. 'Viable projects for unviable farmers – an action research enquiry into the structure and processes of rural poverty in arid regions'. Symposium on Rural Development in South Asia, IUAES Inter Congress, Amsterdam.

Gupta, A., and A. Prakash 1993. 'On internalization of externalities'. Indian Institute of Management, Ahmedabad. Working paper.

Hager, R. 1991. 'Letter to the editor'. *Multinational Monitor*, September 1991.

Hancock, G. 1989. *Lords of Poverty*. New York. Atlantic Monthly Press.

Hardin, G. 1968. 'The tragedy of the commons'. *Science*. 162:1243-48.

Harding, C. 1975. 'Land reform and social conflict in Peru'. In *The Peruvian Experiment: Continuity and Change under Military Rule*, ed. A.F. Lowenthal. Princeton: Princeton University Press.

Hardoy and Satterthwate 1991. 'Environmental problems of the Third World cities: a global issue ignored?' In *Public Administration and Development*, Vol. II.

Harrison, P. 1992. *The Third Revolution: Population, Environment and a Sustainable World*. Harmondsworth: Penguin Books.

—. 1990. 'Too much life on Earth?' *New Scientist*, 19 May.

Hartmann, B. 1987. *Reproductive Rights and Wrongs: The Global Politics of Population Control and Contraceptive Choice*. New York: Harper & Row.

Headrick, D.R. 1990. 'Technological change'. In *The Earth as Transformed by Human Action. Global and Regional Changes in the Biosphere over the Past 300 Years*, eds B.L. Turner, W.C. Clark, R.W. Kates, J.F. Richards, J.T. Mathews and W.B. Meyer. Cambridge: Cambridge University Press with Clark University.

Hecht, S., and A. Cockburn 1990. *The Fate of the Forest: Developers, Destroyers and Defenders of the Amazon*. New York: Harper Collins.

Helpman, E., and P.R. Krugman 1985. *Market Structure and Foreign Trade: Increasing Returns, Imperfect Competition and the International Economy*. Cambridge, MA: MIT Press.

Hines, C. 1990. *Green Protectionism: Halting the Four Horsemen of the Free Trade Apocalypse*. London: Earth Resources Research.

Hogan, L. 1992. 'Journeys and other stories'. In *Columbus and Beyond: Views from Native Americans*, ed. R. Jorgen. Tucson, AZ: Southwest Parks and Monuments Association.

Holling, C.S. 1973. 'Resilience and the stability of ecological systems'. *Annual Review of Ecological Systems* 4:1-24.

—. 1986. 'The resilience of terrestrial ecosystems: local surprise and global change'. In *Sustainable Development of the Biosphere*, eds W.C. Clark and R.E. Munn. International Institute for Applied Systems Analysis, Laxenburg, Austria. Cambridge: Cambridge University Press.

Hueting, R. 1992. 'Growth, environment and national income'. In *Real-Life Economics: Understanding Wealth Creation*, eds P. Ekins and M. Max-Neef. London: Routledge.

Hulme M., and M. Kelly 1993. 'Exploring the links between desertification and climate change'. *Environment* 35:6.

IFAD 1992. *The State of World Rural Poverty: An Inquiry into its Causes and Consequences*. Rome: International Fund for Agricultural Development.

IFPRI-DSE 1991. 'Sustainable Agriculture, Growth and Poverty Alleviation', 23-27 September 1991. Feldafing, Germany.

IISD 1993. *Trade and Sustainable Development: The New Research Agenda*. Winnepeg: International Institute for Sustainable Development.

Jacobson, J. 1988. 'Planning the global family'. In *State of the World 1988*. A Worldwatch Institute Report on Progress Toward a Sustainable Development, eds L.R. Brown *et al.*, 151-69.

Jaganathan, N.V. 1989. 'Poverty, Public Policies and the Environment'. World Bank Environment Working Paper No. 24. Washington, D.C.: The World Bank.

Jayal, N.D. 1985. 'Emerging pattern of the crisis in water resource conservation'. In *Emerging Pattern of the Crisis in Water Resource Conservation*, J. Bondyopadhya, N.D. Jayal, U. Schoettli and C. Singh, ed. Dehra Dun: Natraj Publishers:78-89.

King, S. 1992. 'Pharmaceutical discovery, ethnobotany, tropical forests, and reciprocity: integrating indigenous knowledge, conservation, and sustainable development'. In *Sustainable Harvest and Marketing of Rain Forest Products*, eds M. Plotkin and L. Famolare. Washington, D.C.: Island Press.

Kinloch, D., H. Kuhnlein, and D.C.G. Muir 1992. 'Inuit foods and diet: a preliminary assessment of benefits and risks'. *The Science of the Total Environment*, 122:247-78.

Krugman, P.R. 1990. 'Trade, accumulation and uneven development'. In *Rethinking International Trade*, ed. P.R. Krugman. Cambridge MA: MIT Press.

Lang, T. 1992. *Food fit for the world?* London: SAFE Alliance.

Lange, G.M., and F. Duchin 1993. 'Integrated environmental-economic accounting, natural resource accounts, and natural resource management in Africa'. Institute for Economic Analysis. New York: New York University. Unpublished paper.

Lappe and Schurman 1988. *Taking Population Seriously*. London: Earthscan.

Leonard, H.J., ed. 1989. *Environment and the Poor: Development Strategy for a Common Agenda*. Overseas Development Council, Washington, D.C.. New Brunswick: Transaction Books.

Lucas, R.E., Jr., 1988. 'On the mechanics of economic development'. *Journal of Monetary Economics* 22:3-42.

Lutz, E., and M. Munasinghe 1991. 'Accounting for the environment'. *Finance and Development* March 1991.

Madeley, J. 1992. *Trade and the Poor*. London: Intermediate Technology Publications.

Mansfield, W.H. 1993. *Environmental Capacity Building for Sustainable Development*. Nairobi: United Nations Environment Programme, 10 March 1993.

Martinez-Alier, J. 1991 'Ecology and the poor: a neglected dimension of Latin American history'. *Journal of Latin American Studies* 23:621-39.

—. 1993. 'Distributional obstacles to international environmental policy: the failures at Rio and prospects after Rio'. *Environmental Values* 2:97-124.

Mata, F.J., L. Onisto and J.R. Vallentyne 1994. 'Consumption: the other side of population for development'. Paper prepared for the International Conference on Population and Development.

Maybury-Lewis, D. 1992. *Millennium: Tribal Wisdom and the Modern World*. New York: Viking Press.

Meadows, D. 1988. 'Quality of life'. In *Earth-88: Changing Geographic Perspectives*. Washington, D.C.: National Geographic Society.

Meltzoff, S.K., and E. LiPuma 1986. 'The social and political economy of coastal zone management: shrimp mariculture in Ecuador'. *Coastal Zone Management Journal* 14:349-80.

Ministry of Environment and Forests, India 1994. *Report of the Expert Group on People's Participation in Joint Forest Management*. Government of India.

Mitsch, W.J. 1991. 'Ecological engineering: approaches to sustainability and biodiversity in the U.S. and China'. In *Ecological Economics: The Science and Management of Sustainability*, ed. R. Costanza. New York: Columbia University Press.

Moran, E.F. 1993. *Through Amazonian Eyes: the Human Ecology of Amazonian Populations*. Iowa City: University of Iowa Press.

Muir, D.C.G., R. Wagemann, B.T. Hargrave, D.J. Thomas, D.B. Peakall and R.J. Norstrom 1992. 'Arctic marine ecosystem contamination'. *The Science of the Total Environment* 122:75-134.

Munasinghe, M., and E. Lutz 1991. 'Environmental-economic evaluation of projects and policies for sustainable development'. World Bank Environment Department Working Paper No. 42. Washington, D.C.: The World Bank.

Murra, J.V. 1973. 'Rite and crop in the Inca state'. In *Peoples and Cultures of Native South America*, ed. D.R. Gross. American Museum of Natural History. Garden City, New York: Doubleday/The Natural History Press.

Myers, N. 1989. *Deforestation Rates in Tropical Countries and their Climatic Implications*. London: Friends of the Earth.

Narayana, V.V.D., and G. Sastry 1985. 'Soil conservation in India'. In *Soil Conservation in India*, eds S.A. El-Swaify, W.C. Moldenhauer and A. Lo. Ankeny: Soil Conservation Society of America.

Nash, N.C. 1993. 'Chile advances in a war on poverty, and one million mouths say amen'. *New York Times*, 4 April.

Netting, R. McC. 1993. *Smallholders, Householders: Farm Families and the Ecology of Intensive, Sustainable Agriculture*. Stanford, CA: Stanford University Press.

Norgaard, R.B. 1989. 'The case for methodological pluralism'. *Ecological Economics* 1:37-58.

NRC 1993. *Setting Priorities for Land Conservation*. National Research Council. Washington D.C.: National Academy Press.

O'Connor, M. 1992. 'Value system contests and the appropriation of ecological capital'. Paper presented at the 2nd meeting of the International Society for Ecological Economics, Stockholm.

OECD 1993. *Core Set of Indicators for Environmental Performance Reviews*. Paris: OECD/GD/(93)179.

Opschoor, J.B. 1991. 'GNP and sustainable income measures: some problems and a way out'. In *In Search of Indicators of Sustainable Development*, eds Kuik, Onno and H. Verbruggen. Dordrecht: Kluwer: 39-45.

Opschoor, J.B. 1992. 'Sustainable development, the economic process and economic analysis'. In *Environment, Economy and Sustainable Development*, ed. J.B. Opschoor. Groningen: Wolters-Noordhoff: 25-52.

Opschoor, J.B. and L. Reijnders 1991. 'Towards sustainable development indicators'. In *In Search of Indicators of Sustainable Development*, eds Kuik, Onno and H. Verbruggen. Dordrecht: Kluwer: 7-29.

Opschoor J.B., A. de Savornin Lohman and J.B. Vos 1994. *Managing the Environment: The Role of Economic Instruments*. Paris: OECD.

Opschoor, J.B., and R.K. Turner 1994. 'Environmental economics and environmental policy instruments'. In *Economic Incentives and Environmental Policies: Principles and Practice*, eds J.B. Opschoor and R.K. Turner. Dordrecht: Kluwer/European Science Foundation: 1-39.

Ostrom, E., L. Schroeder and S. Wynne 1993. *Institutional Incentives and Sustainable Development. Infrastructure Policies in Perspective*. Boulder: Westview Press.

Oxfam 1993a. *Debt-for-Nature Failures. Oxfam America Update: Amazon*. Boston: Oxfam America.

—. 1993b. *Oxfam America Update: Amazon: The Amazon is Our Life*. Boston: Oxfam America.

—. 1993c. *People-based Development Means Empowerment. Oxfam America Update: Amazon*. Boston: Oxfam America.

Parikh, J., and Kirit, S.G. *et al.* 1991. 'Consumption patterns, the driving force of environmental stress', Research Discussion Paper No. 59. Bombay: Indira Gandhi Institute of Development.

Pearce, D., and K. Turner 1990. *Economics of Natural Resources and the Environment*. Hemel Hempstead: Harvester Wheatsheaf.

Pearce, D.W., and J.J. Warford 1992. *World Without End: Economics, Environment and Sustainable Development*. Oxford: Oxford University Press for The World Bank.

Perelman, M. 1976. 'Efficiency in agriculture: the economics of energy'. In *Radical Agriculture*, ed. R. Merrill. New York: Harper Colophon Books.

Perrings, C., and J.B. Opschoor 1994. 'The loss of biodiversity: some policy implications'. *Environment and Resource Economics* 4 (1):1-13.

Peskin H., and E. Lutz 1990 'A survey of resource and environmental accounting in industrialized countries'. World Bank Environment Department Working Paper No. 37. Washington, D.C.: The World Bank.

Pimentel, D. *et al.* 1987. 'World agriculture and soil erosion'. *BioScience* 37:277-83.

Pimentel, D., M.A. Moran, S. Fast, G. Weber, R. Bukantis, L. Baillet, P. Bovering, S. Hindman and M. Young 1981. 'Biomass energy from crop and forestry residues'. *Science* 212:1110-5.

Platt, J. 1973. 'Social traps'. *American Psychologist* 28:642-51.

Plotkin, M.J. 1988. 'The outlook for new agricultural and industrial products from the tropics'. In *Biodiversity*, ed. E.O. Wilson. Washington D.C.: National Academy Press.

Primavera, J.H. 1995. 'A critical review of shrimp pond culture in the Philippines'. *Reviews in Fisheries Science*. In press.

Rahman, A. 1993. Testimony presented by Atiq Rahman, director of the Bangladesh Center for Advanced Studies, to a subcommittee of the U.S. Congress, Committee on Banking, Finance and Urban Affairs. 3 August 1993.

Rahman, A., N. Robins and A. Roncerel, eds 1993. *Exploding the Population Myth. Consumption versus Population – Which is the Climate Bomb?* Brussels, Dhaka, Rome, Santiago: Climate Action Network.

Reed, D., ed. 1992. *Structural Adjustment and the Environment*. London: Earthscan.

Rees, W.E. 1992. 'Appropriated carrying capacity: measuring the natural capital requirements of the human economy'. Paper at the ISEE Conference, Stockholm.

Repetto, R. 1992. 'Earth in balance sheet: incorporating natural resources in national income accounts'. *Environment* 34(7): 12-20, 43-5.

—. 1991. *Accounts Overdue: Natural Resource Depreciation in Costa Rica.* Washington D.C.: World Resources Institute.

—. 1987. *The Forest for the Trees? Government Policies and the Misuse of Forest Resources.* Washington, D.C.: World Resources Institute.

—. 1986. *Skimming the Water: Rent-Seeking and the Performance of Public Irrigation Systems.* Washington, D.C.: World Resources Institute.

—. 1985. *Paying the Price: Pesticide Subsidies in Developing Countries.* Washington, D.C.: World Resources Institute.

—. 1979. *Economic Equality and Fertility in Developing Countries*. Baltimore: Johns Hopkins University Press.

Repetto, R., W.B. Magrath, M. Wells, C. Beer and F. Rossini 1989. *Wasting Assets: Natural Resources in the National Income Accounts*. Washington, D.C.: World Resources Institute.

Revelle, R. 1976. 'The resources available for agriculture'. *Scientific American* September 1976: 165-78.

Rich, B. 1994. *Mortgaging the Earth: The World Bank, Environmental Impoverishment, and the Crisis of Development*. Boston: Beacon Press.

Ritchie, M. 1993. 'Agricultural trade liberalization: implications for sustainable agriculture'. In *The Case Against Free Trade: GATT, NAFTA, and the Globalization of Corporate Power*, eds R. Nader *et al.* Earth Island Press and North Atlantic Books.

Ritchie, M. 1992. 'Free trade versus sustainable agriculture: the implications of NAFTA'. *The Ecologist*, 22:221-27.

Robertson, D. 1972. *International Trade Policy*. London: Macmillan.

Rodda, A. 1991. *Women and the Environment*. New Jersey: Zed Books.

Ropke, I. 1995. 'Trade, development and sustainability. A critical assessment of the "free trade dogma"'. *Ecological Economics*. In press.

Ruitenbeek, H.J. 1991. *Mangrove Management: An Economic Analysis of Management Options with a Focus on Bintuni Bay, Irian Jaya*. Prepared for Environmental Management Development in Indonesia Project. Jakarta and Halifax: Dalhousie University.

—. 1991. 'The role of indicators in the decision process'. In *Economic, Ecological and Decision Theories: Indicators of Ecologically Sustainable Development*, eds P.A. Victor, J.J. Kay and H.J. Ruitenbeek. Canadian Environmental Advisory Council. Ottawa: Environment Canada.

Samuelson, P.A. 1969. 'The gains from international trade once again. In *International Trade*, ed. J. Bhagwati. Harmondsworth: Penguin.

—. 1962. 'The gains from international trade once again'. *Economic Journal* 72:820-9.

—. 1961. *Economics: An Introductory Analysis*. 5th ed. New York: McGraw Hill.

Sanchez, V., M. Castillejos and L. Rojas Bracho 1989. *Población, recursos y medio ambiente en México*. A.C. Mexico: Fundación Universo Veintiuno.

Segura, O., and J. Boyce 1994. 'Investing in natural and human capital in developing countries'. In *Investing in Natural Capital*, eds A.-M. Jansson, C. Folke, M. Hammer and R. Costanza. Washington, D.C.: ISEE/Island Press.

Sen, G., and K. Gowen, eds 1988. *Development Alternatives for Women in a New Era*.

Shipton, P.M. 1988. 'The Kenyan land tenure reform: misunderstandings in the public creation of private property'. In *Land and Society in Contemporary Africa*, eds R.E. Downs and S.P. Reyna. Hanover, NH: University Press of New England.

Shkilnyk, A.M. 1985. *A Poison Stronger Than Love. The Destruction of an Ojibwa Community*. New Haven and London: Yale University Press.

Shrybman, S. 1990. 'Free trade vs. the environment: the implications of GATT'. *The Ecologist* 20:30-4.

Siebert, H. 1982. 'Nature as a life support system'. *Journal of Economics* 42 (2):133-42.

Solow, R. 1992. *An Almost Practical Step Toward Sustainability*. Washington, D.C.: Resources for the Future.

Solow, R. 1991. 'Growth theory'. In *Companion to Contemporary Economic Thought*, eds D. Greenaway, M. Bleaney and I.M.T. Stewart. London: Routledge.

Somma, M. 1991. 'Ecological flight: explaining the move from country to city in developing nations'. *Environmental History Review* 15 (Fall 1991):3.

Southgate, D. 1992. 'Shrimp mariculture development in Ecuador: some resource policy issues'. Working Paper 5, EPAT/MUSIA-Research and Training University of Wisconsin-Madison.

Srinivasan, K. 1993. 'Demographic transition in India since 1970, trends and correlates'. Background Paper, Second India Reassessment Project. Washington, D.C.: World Resources Institute.

Steininger, K. 1994. 'Reconciling trade and environment: towards a comparative advantage for long-term policy goals'. *Ecological Economics*.

Strange, M. 1988. *Family Farming: A New Economic Vision*. Lincoln: University of Nebraska Press.

Swaminathan, M.S. 1988. 'Global agriculture at the crossroads'. In *Earth-88: Changing Geographic Perspectives*. Washington, D.C.: National Geographic Society.

Teger, A.I. 1980. *Too Much Invested to Quit*. New York: Pergamon Press.

The Economist 1992. 'Let them eat pollution'. The Economist, 8 February: 66.

Tolba, M.K., O.A. El-Kholy, E. El-Hinnawi, M.W. Holdgate, D.F. McMichael and R.E. Munn 1992. *The World Environment, 1972-1992: Two Decades of Challenge*. London: Chapman & Hall, on behalf of the United Nations Environment Programme.

UN 1992. *World Economic Survey 1992*. New York: United Nations.

—. 1973. 'The determinants and consequences of population trends'. *United Nations Population Studies* No. 50. New York: United Nations.

UNCED: Agenda 21.

UNCTAD, 1992. 'Commodities: a struggle to survive'. Paper UNCTAD/PSM/ CAS/380/Add.12. Geneva: UNCTAD.

UNDP 1993. *Human Development Report 1993*. New York: Oxford University Press.

—. 1992. *Human Development Report 1992*. New York: Oxford University Press.

—. 1991. *Human Development Report 1991*. Oxford University Press.

UNEP 1992. *Strengthening National Institution Capabilities For Sustainable Development*. New York: United Nations Environment Programme.

—. 1991. *Status of Desertification and Implementation of the United Nations Plan of Action to Combat Desertification*. Nairobi: United Nations Environment Programme.

UNFPA 1993. *The State of World Population 1993*. New York: United Nations Population Fund.

UNICEF 1993. *State of the World's Children 1993*. Oxford University Press for UNICEF.

Venkateswarlu, J. 1985. 'Ecological crises in agroecosystems'. In *Ecological Crises in Agroecosystems*, J. Bondyopadhya, N.D. Jayal, U. Schoettli and C. Singh, ed. Dehra Dun: Natraj Publishers: 91-109.

Verbruggen, H. and H.M.A. Jansen 1995. 'International coordination of environmental policies. In *Principles of Environmental and Resource Economics*, eds H. Folmer, L. Gable and H. Opschoor. Cheltenham: Edward Elgar (forthcoming).

WDR 1992. *World Development Report: Development and the Environment*. Washington, D.C.: The World Bank.

—. 1990. *World Development Report: Poverty*. Washington D.C.: The World Bank.

Wells, P., and Jetter, M. 1992. *The Global Consumer*. London: Victor Gollancz.

Weterings, R. and J.B. Opschoor 1994. *Towards Environmental Performance Indicators Based on the Notion of Environmental Space.* Ryswyk, Netherlands: RMNO.

White, R.R. 1993. *North, South, and the Environmental Crisis.* Toronto: University of Toronto Press.

Whitmore, *et al.* 1990. 'Long-term population change'. In *The Earth as Transformed by Human Action: Global and Regional Changes in the Biosphere over the Past 300 Years*, eds B.L. Turner II, *et al.* New York: Cambridge University Press with Clark University.

WHO 1992. *Our Planet, Our Health.* Report of the WHO Commission on Health and Environment. Geneva: World Health Organization.

Williams, M. 1990. 'Forests'. In *The Earth as Transformed by Human Action*, B.L. Turner II, R.W. Kates, J.F. Richards, J.T. Mathews and W.B. Meyer. New York: Cambridge University Press with Clark University.

Wood, B. and H.A. Patrinos 1993. 'Bolivia'. In 'Indigenous people and poverty in Latin America: an empirical analysis', eds G. Psacharopoulos and H.A. Patrinos. Preliminary paper, The World Bank, Latin America and the Caribbean Technical Department, Regional Studies Program.

World Bank 1993. *Poverty Reduction Handbook.* Washington, D.C.: The World Bank.

—. 1992. The World Bank Environment Division. *The World Bank and the Environment.* Washington, D.C.: The World Bank.

WCED 1987. *Our Common Future.* Oxford: Oxford University Press.

WRI 1994-95. World Resources Institute. *World Resources, People and the Environment.* New York: Oxford University Press.

World Resources Institute, IUCN–The World Conservation Union and the United Nations Environment Programme 1992. *Global Biodiversity Strategy. Guidelines for Action to Save, Study, and Use Earth's Biotic Wealth Sustainably and Equitably.*

Yudelman, M. 1989. 'Sustainable and equitable development in irrigated environments'. In *Environment and the Poor: Development Strategies for a Common Agenda*, eds. Leonard *et al.*